Pedagogical Theory of Wisdom Literature

Pedagogical Theory of Wisdom Literature

An Application of Educational Theory to Biblical Texts

ADRIAN E. HINKLE

with a contribution by Rebecca D. Webster

WIPF & STOCK · Eugene, Oregon

PEDAGOGICAL THEORY OF WISDOM LITERATURE
An Application of Educational Theory to Biblical Texts

Copyright © 2017 Adrian E. Hinkle. All rights reserved. Except for brief quotations in critical publications or reviews, no part of this book may be reproduced in any manner without prior written permission from the publisher. Write: Permissions, Wipf and Stock Publishers, 199 W. 8th Ave., Suite 3, Eugene, OR 97401.

Wipf & Stock
An Imprint of Wipf and Stock Publishers
199 W. 8th Ave., Suite 3
Eugene, OR 97401

www.wipfandstock.com

PAPERBACK ISBN: 978-1-4982-2864-0
HARDCOVER ISBN: 978-1-4982-2866-4
EBOOK ISBN: 978-1-4982-2865-7

Manufactured in the U.S.A.   MARCH 10, 2017

"Scripture quotations taken from the New American Standard Bible®, Copyright © 1960, 1962, 1963, 1968, 1971, 1972, 1973, 1975, 1977, 1995 by The Lockman Foundation Used by permission." (www.Lockman.org)

To Leland, I love you deeply.

Contents

Preface | ix

Introduction | 1

Chapter 1
Active Learning | 12

Chapter 2
A Literary Approach | 29

Chapter 3
Pedagogy and the Construction of Childhood | 45

Chapter 4
Pedagogy of Job | 61

Chapter 5
Pedagogy of Proverbs | 80

Chapter 6
Pedagogy of Ecclesiastes | 98

Chapter 7
Pedagogy of Song of Songs | 114

Chapter 8
Summary | 126

Bibliography | 147

Preface

WITHIN THE HEART OF each of us, God has placed a sense of something eternal and a desire to seek after it. "This quest is a deep-seated desire, a compulsive drive, because man is made in the image of God to appreciate the beauty of creation (on an aesthetic level); to know the character, composition, and meaning of the world (on an academic and philosophical level); and to discern its purpose and destiny (on a theological level) [. . .] Man has an inborn inquisitiveness and capacity to learn how everything in his experience can be integrated to make a whole."[1]

Though the Hebrew Bible is didactic in nature, the means by which it informs readers how to teach others is largely overlooked. When we read scripture, we often rightly focus on how God is revealed to humanity. Yet, in addition to God revealing himself to humanity, it is argued here that the writers also recorded how to continue teaching others about God.

This book advocates that the writers of the wisdom corpus included specific references that inform the readers how to continue teaching the religious ethos recorded within the Hebrew Bible. Those who take full advantage of these instructions put into action the specific means by which religious education is introduced within these texts. It is my intent to draw attention to the abundant references for religious instructions for others to consider their ongoing importance in modern religious training.

This book is intended for broad readership of those interested in this subject. Therefore, this book is written with an expectation that there are many readers who are without knowledge of the original Hebrew language. Though there are occasional references to the Hebrew, these references are made explicit as is the importance of the full explanation of the words' usage. On the occasion that I do include the Hebrew references, a translation is included to ensure each reader has full access and ability to clearly follow the argument and importance of the word within biblical text.

1. Kaiser, *Ecclesiastes*, 66.

It is admitted that this study uses a somewhat eclectic hermeneutical approach that combines grammatical-historical and literary criticism to draw attention to nuances within the texts. I am sympathetic to readers who are not accustomed to these approaches and many readers who are fortunate enough to have formal training in exegesis are likely only trained in grammatical-historical interpretive methods. Thus, these readers cling closely the historical critical matters. However, it is my opinion that vital aspects of the biblical texts are not fully regarded when only viewing these texts through a single lens. Literary criticism is just as vital an exercise in the examination of the biblical texts as it highlights the focus of the texts. It also causes readers to ask probing questions on the irregularities of the text and determine the significance of their inclusion. These interpretive matters will be discussed at length throughout the book. Readers unaccustomed to literary criticism may hesitate to agree in some areas. However, if I may strongly assert here my affirmation of the fully inerrant and authoritative word of God and assure readers of my presupposition that all of scripture is fully inspired. As the verbal plenary inspiration theory allows, I also contend that this inspiration also covers the full process of recording and revising of the biblical texts. This too, will be discussed further in chapter 2.

I have much gratitude for my family, pastors, professors, and colleagues who challenge my thinking and encourage me to pursue my passion for biblical literature. I am especially thankful for Dr. Ann Jeffers at Heythrop College, University of London, who strongly encouraged me to go further in my examination of the construction of childhood in my research in pedagogical theory. I also appreciate Okoro Ifeoma Favour, my former graduate student, who helped me immensely with some of the early research on the construction of childhood. I am also pleased to share my research with my dear friend and colleague, Dr. Rebecca Webster. I am indebted to her expertise in educational psychology and social learning theory. I have greatly enjoyed our animated discussions on our research and anticipate future collaborative works.

Introduction

THE DISTINCTION OF WISDOM Literature is often treated by scholars as a special phenomenon within the Hebrew Bible. The writing style of this genre is a unifying feature between the Israelite nation and its near eastern neighbors. Its didactic properties are rarely contested and attempts to concisely define it often fall short. There is no greater word that describes the interaction of Yahweh and humanity better than teacher. One could argue the entire role of Scripture is to reveal God and his relationship to humanity. Worded differently, it is God teaching humanity about himself and how humanity can interact with him. It is certainly agreed that there are many roles of God. Yet, one of the fundamental roles we repeatedly observe in Scripture is his interaction with humanity as he instructs and corrects.

The rationale for this study is the existing research gap between studies completed on religious education in Israel and learning theory models. In response to this gap, this book primarily focuses on three areas: religious education in Israel in correlation with their construction of childhood, evidence of religious instruction in Wisdom Literature, and the correlation between these sample texts and modern learning theory.

As I lay the foundation needed for showing the correlation in teaching and Wisdom Literature, I first focus on active learning with a specific focus on social cognitive learning. Social learning is well established outside of biblical literature. The recognition of social learning is the notable learning that occurs in a social context through observation. While there is considerable scholarship available on social learning, it is a relatively new area of study in application to the Hebrew Bible.

Likewise, the construction of childhood is also a relatively new field of research within biblical studies. While the period of childhood and its contrasting characteristics from adulthood is identifiable, this period is not fixed and varies indiscriminately between places and cultures.

There is considerable variation on the age and responsibilities assigned to "children." Here, I also build on the prior research established by Henry Marrou and James Crenshaw. Marrou contributes considerable research through his study of formal education systems. However, his focus is primarily on non-religious education and concentrates on people groups that occur later than those described within Wisdom Literature. Furthermore, his main argument is for the existence of formal education. He does not directly address how education takes place. Likewise, Crenshaw has made substantial contributions to biblical research in his studies on religious education. He acknowledges that religious education occurred in the home and was likely not part of the formal education system. Like Marrou, he focuses on the support for formal education and scribal schools. He, too, does not address the means by which religious education occurs. Therefore, the research contained in this book does not argue for the validity or historical existence of formal education. Instead, the focus is distinctly on religious education and the pedagogical features contained within Wisdom Literature that describe *how* religious education is expected to take place. Rather than debating the existence of educational systems, literary analysis is used to focus on textual evidence for instructions or examples of religious education.

These two areas (learning theory and construction of childhood) are then used as several Wisdom texts are discussed in respect to their distinct inclusion of pedagogical features that illustrate how religious training occurred. Here I will explore the use of nature, tradition, Torah, and social communities as part of the tools for educating young learners.

DELIMITATIONS OF SCOPE AND KEY ASSUMPTIONS

The discussion is limited to the four books of the Wisdom corpus (Job, Proverbs, Ecclesiastes, and Song of Songs) when examining the key areas of social learning and pedagogical features. I limit the research of this book to Wisdom Literature because of my earlier work in *Pedagogical Theory of the Hebrew Bible* (2016), where I investigate the examples of pedagogical features within the Pentateuch and Deuteronomistic history with reference to the conceptual framework for active learning and learning styles introduced by Howard Gardner and Neil Fleming.

Within this study, Wisdom Literature is examined in its final canonical form. Based on observations of these texts, descriptions of pedagogical features are then compared against the existing research for active and social learning theories in order to determine specific patterns in the pedagogical features contained in Wisdom Literature. Because of peculiarities in its genre and compilation, Psalms is also examined in a separate study.

The data collected does not include the further treatment of texts published in Jewish literature such as the Mishnah nor do I debate issues of historicity relating to Israel. Questions regarding the relationship of the final form of Wisdom Literature and the oral tradition and literary formation of the texts are beyond the scope of this study. While this study does not argue for the historicity of Israel, it does examine the biblical texts in light of the social contexts as described within the Hebrew Canon. The links between Wisdom Literature and the Pentateuch are also discussed, though they are limited to specific references as applicable to the immediate context of the argument. Although limited in use, these links show the ongoing relationship of the distinctive worldview and contribute to the evidence for the social and pedagogical features included within Wisdom Literature.

This study remains limited to the biblical Wisdom texts and does not include discussions from wisdom texts outside of the Wisdom corpus. One rationale for this limitation is the wider debate on the function of sages and influences of the multifaceted social constructs that impact the writings of extrabiblical accounts. Furthermore, the argument is not expanded to biblical literature outside of the Wisdom texts because of the recognition of the complexity in which the wisdom writing style is integrated in several biblical genres. Including these texts does not add enough value to the argument to warrant their inclusion nor would it change the conclusions made.

The rationale for separating Wisdom Literature from my previous study on the Pentateuch and Deuteronomistic History is the recognition of a distinct change in the pedagogical features included in the narratives verses wisdom writing. Because of the special nuances associated with the pedagogy of Wisdom Literature, I felt it was necessary to separate these two studies to best address their unique features. It is also broadly accepted to study Wisdom corpus as a literary distinction because of its own theological peculiarities, such as the lack of reference to salvation history, covenantal relationship between Israel and Yahweh, and Yahweh's self-revelation to Israel.

Definitions

Education

There is a fundamental distinction between education and pedagogy. While these words share similar features, they are not synonymous. As used in this study, education refers to the entire process of communicating knowledge from one person to another. In the larger social context, education not only includes the transferal of intellectual knowledge, but also includes the social and religious constructs that are passed from one generation to the next. Education is the direct product of the actions and transfer of knowledge from an instructor to a learner.

Under the broad definition of education is the distinction between formal and informal education. Formal education is the conventional transfer of knowledge though a planned, systematic manner that occurs in a social context of a greater ratio of learners to instructor. In contrast, informal education occurs through shared experience. It is not necessarily conducted in a systematic or orderly way through pre-planned lessons. Instead, it occurs through casual interaction and participation in social activities that influence younger members of a community in the development of their worldview and social/religious expectations.

The biblical texts do not include specific references to formal educational systems which leave readers to conclude that they were either non-existent or so well recognized that there was no need to reference them in the preserved accounts. Instead, the references for instruction primarily occur within the immediate social context of the family such as the command to instruct one's children in Exod. 13:14 and Deut. 11:19. Descriptions of informal education also occur in social settings through the observations of other members of the community, as observed in Prov. 23:26. In the occasions of an amassed group for instruction, these gatherings are described as impromptu instead of carefully pre-planned lesson as described in Joel 1:14 and Exod. 3:16. In these examples, Israel is described as engaging in diverse approaches of communication with varied intended outcomes. There are few references in the Hebrew Bible of oral instruction that is not directly linked to either an observable pedagogical feature or kinesthetic learning activity. Recognizing its need to preserve its historical and religious heritage, Israel not only preserved its traditions but also included the specific means for educating young children and alien converts to the Israelite faith tradition. This concept of informal education encompassed all aspects of community life and supports the evidence of Israel's ability to retain its religious ethos in the training of each successive generation. At its core, education is the communication and transferal of social, intellectual, and religious knowledge from one person to another.

Pedagogy

Within the scope of education, exists pedagogy. Peter Mortimore describes pedagogy as, "any conscious activity by one person designed to enhance learning in another."[1] In short, education is concerned with *what* a student learns while pedagogy is concerned with *how* the student learns. It is the specific method of instruction or teaching strategy. It is also recognized that pedagogy is still an ongoing debate among scholars in the field of education as is the distinct learning characteristics of children and adults. Because of their different needs in learning, the term andragogy was developed to refer to the specific accommodations needed for adult learners while pedagogy is used to refer to the strategies for teaching children. However, pedagogy is also used as a universal term that can refer to the teaching techniques for both adults and children. Therefore, the research in this study will limit itself to the use of the term pedagogy for the sake of simplicity, though it will include an examination of teaching methods that pertain to both children and adults. Evidence from the biblical texts will defend that the writers of Wisdom Literature articulated a specific instruction method for teaching children and adult faith adherents within their community.

Pedagogy considers this method of instruction. In addition to methodology, it focuses on the relationship between the instructor and learner as well as the environment or location for learning. The format for instruction is frequently classified as learning styles. A learning style is, "the composite of characteristic cognitive, affective, and physiological factors that serve as relatively stable indicators of how a learner perceives, interacts with, and responds to the learning environment."[2] The definition and efficiency for learning styles are strongly debated and criticized between scholars in the fields of education and psychology. This study will not attempt to neutralize these arguments. They will, however, be further discussed as they relate to defining the pedagogical characteristics included in Wisdom Literature.

1. Mortimore, *Understanding Pedagogy*, 17.
2. Furnham, *The Psychology of Behaviour At Work*, 189.

Ethos

An ethos is a culture or philosophical worldview that defines an individual or community group. It is observable through a combination of the communication and actions between individuals. An ethos influences the presuppositions and values protected by an individual or community. It also influences the reputation and integrity of the individual or group as well as their focus for expertise.

CONTRIBUTION TO BIBLICAL RESEARCH

The contribution of this research is the investigation of pedagogical features within Wisdom Literature with reference to the conceptual framework for active learning and subcategories introduced by Howard Gardner and Neil Fleming. There are several studies available documenting the importance of educational theory. Studies that address educational systems in time periods like those described in Wisdom Literature typically focus on formal education and seek to offer historical evidence of these schools. However, they do not address pedagogy. Prior to the research for this book, educational theory has not been substantially applied to Wisdom Literature. It is observable that the Israelite faith community assumes responsibility for educating its youth on the culture's social and religious expectations. Though the Wisdom corpus does not offer an unambiguous text that addresses how the community educated the adults, youth, and resident aliens, the descriptions of religious events and processes used for conveying religious ethos and mythos are included in numerous example texts. Examination of these texts offers examples of the instructional methods. Similar but distinct from the narratives of the Pentateuch and Deuteronomistic History, Wisdom Literature uses tangible experiences and kinesthetic learning environments that create active learning engagement. Though the teaching itself is dialogical, it occurs in the context that provokes curiosity.

This study addresses the lack of published research pertaining to Israel's pedagogy for religious education. Biblical passages from the Wisdom corpus were selected based on their description of pedagogical features. Biblical passages included in this study are examined to determine the pedagogical approach observed in each scene as well as the underlying principles behind the human behaviors encountered in the learning situations recorded in Wisdom Literature. These texts were then analyzed against existing studies relating to active and social learning theories to determine their categorization. Where pertinent, limited discussions are included for the editorial revisions of the biblical text to highlight where later editors altered the text to better emphasize the pedagogical features. The advantage of this method is the control of the scope of literature required for study. Early in this research, a clearly established pattern of social learning is confirmed and discussed to support the incorporation of observations and transfer of knowledge as a formalized pedagogy for religious education in Wisdom Literature. In education, the transfer of knowledge refers to the learning acquired in one context that is applied to another. It is the ability to apply knowledge to new situations.

The intention is to investigate whether the specific means for religious education was purposefully included in Wisdom Literature, in its current final form. Biblical texts that include specific descriptions of pedagogy were selected for further investigation and comparison against educational models for active and social learning. The purpose of this investigation is to prove the intentional inclusion of pedagogy for religious education within the present final form of Wisdom Literature. The dominant pedagogical examples recorded in my previous study on the Pentateuch and Deuteronomistic History are visual and kinesthetic. However, this pattern changes in Wisdom Literature. Here, the dominant pedagogy is social learning and the transfer of knowledge from observed behavior or observed patterns in nature to a religious context. These pedagogical features are utilized to reinforce behaviors and religious expectations taught in other biblical texts of the Hebrew Bible. Therefore, the active, experiential learning theories of social learning discussed in modern education studies are modeled and described within Wisdom Literature. The conclusion is that the writers and editor(s) purposefully bring the readers' attention to these pedagogical features so that later audiences would likewise model this pedagogy for religious training.

ORDER

The first three chapters of this book lay out the foundational background knowledge pertaining to the learning theories and the construction of childhood. While there are several studies available for learning styles, both Howard Gardner and Neil Fleming remain two of the most influential contributors in their field. Chapter 1 summarizes some of their research and gives the rational for using Flemming's terminology throughout this study. This chapter also defines the second major learning style discussed throughout the book, social cognitive learning. The roles of active learning and the means by which it is represented within the biblical texts are examined in the chapters that follow.

Chapter 2 lays the necessary foundation for the literary approach of this study. While there are multiple sound approaches for exegetical work, the literary approach more adequately discloses the recorded pedagogical features than other hermeneutical methods. This chapter will also summarize some of the existing scholarly contributions of authorship and editorial activity within Wisdom Literature, as it communicates their suppositions toward relating their own ethos as normative and contributive for future audiences. The lack of scholarly consensus regarding the historical reliability of the stories contained in Wisdom Literature complicates the discussion of the pedagogical features. Since arguing the historicity of the biblical texts is beyond the scope of this research, the literary approach best validates the role of these pedagogical features without becoming caught up in debating the historical authenticity. The literary approach also validates the presence of instructional methodology and determines if is emphasized within the text in contribution to the overall discussion of the means by which religious instruction is described within Wisdom Literature.

Chapter 3 provides the conceptual framework for social learning theory within the overall context of the construction of childhood. As a relatively new field of interest in the biblical studies, this important research is significant in contributing to the overall recognition of how children were taught and their relationship within the community in which they lived. It also provides insight into why elders seek to educate younger generations as a means for ensuring their livelihood and increase social status. The expectations and prominent patterns for thinking and modeling behavior have substantial impact on the overall discussion with relationship to pedagogy.

Chapters 4–7 examine specific texts within the final canonical form of Wisdom Literature with discussion relating to the pedagogical features. Each reference or example of instruction is discussed in light of learning theories and classified accordingly. Each of these chapters examines the texts in relationship to the use of nature, tradition, the Pentateuch and the social context in their teaching methodologies. The research contained in these chapters will support a strong inclusion of pedagogical features that directly relate to visual, kinesthetic, and social learning within the broader conceptual framework of active learning. The instructional patterns are distinct and often interrelate with one another.

Since the Wisdom corpus is often the primary literature studied when examining teaching and learning, the instruction in the Writings with a comparison to the Pentateuch will be examined as a brief area for study in chapters 4–7. Gerald Sheppard has already exposed the concept of Wisdom Literature used as "a theological category associated with an understanding of canon which formed a perspective from which to interpret Torah [. . .]."[3] Chapters 4–7 will examine the examples of pedagogy recorded in Wisdom Literature and discuss its relationship with active and social learning theories. Within the Wisdom corpus, writers utilize nature as a pedagogical tool to teach religious ethos. One example explored is Yahweh's providential control of nature as illustrated in Job 38–41 where the writer illustrates this ethos through the object lessons of sun, sea, ox, and steed. Fundamental truths related to humanity are vicariously taught to Job and later to readers of this account through the observations of these four elements from nature. Proverbs also pulls examples from nature to better relate patterns expected in social contexts. Sample texts such as Prov. 30:24–28 illustrate these desired traits by drawing similarities from insects and animals. Ecclesiastes similarly draws from the cycles within nature as a means for relating the abstract and intangible characteristics of Yahweh through the observable features within nature. The imagery in Song of Songs is replete with illustrations from nature that entices the reader's senses in invokes active learning through engaging the imagination.

These chapters also discuss Wisdom Literature's incorporation of religious tradition and select concepts from the Pentateuch as part of the pedagogical influences. These are discussed through the roles of the dialogues of Job's three friends, Qoheleth's monologue in Ecclesiastes, and the themes such as retribution and justice that are significantly represented in Proverbs.

Last, chapters 4–7 examine the prolific use of social cognitive learning within Wisdom Literature. The instructional value of this learning model will be strongly argued through all four books discussed. In several cases, such as Job and Song of Songs, this reasonably impacts the readers on two levels. First, they observe the learning of the characters

---

3. Shepperd, *Wisdom as a Hermeneutical Construct*, 13.

through social interaction. Second, drawing on Dewey's recognition of imagination in learning (discussed in chapter 1), the readers also vicariously learn as they experience the texts alongside the characters.

Finally, chapter 8 summarizes the research of this study. It will briefly synthesize the data results into a formal conclusion for review as well as indicate potential ongoing research in this subject. In summary, active and social learning theories and the literary approach for biblical research is used in this deductive study of Wisdom Literature. This will support the claim of the intentional inclusion of specific pedagogical features for ongoing religious education.

A close examination of the Wisdom corpus reveals a specific pedagogical pattern used throughout each book. The "telling" of the narrator or the "showing" through the actions of the characters are examples of the work of the narrator to include specific details that impact the reader. The Wisdom texts consistently use a combination of telling and showing when including the examples for religious training. The narrator is synonymous with writer and is described by Jan Fokkelman the veritable ringmaster who allows readers to "hear" the voices from the characters whom he allows to speak.[4] It is therefore asserted that the biblical writers write with didactic intentions. They include specific details within their texts that draw readers' attention and point them toward making appropriate conclusions or drawing inferences from the details of the texts. Included in this are the details pertaining to religious instructions and the specific examples and illustrations of how teachers taught.

In summary of the argument, this study identifies three areas of focus, religious education in Israel in correlation with their construction of childhood, examples of religious instruction in Wisdom Literature, and the correlation between these sample texts and modern learning theory. Within the context of Job, it will be noted that the invisible becomes visible through the incorporation of story and imagination. In Proverbs, the pedagogy is strongly rooted in the social context. "[. . .] it is clear that the community precedes the individual person, that the community begins by stating its parameters and the perceptual field in which the new person must live and grow."[5] Here, the intangible law is touched through the ability of the learner to observe both the rewards and consequences of obedience and disobedience through the actions

---

4. Fokkelman, *Reading*, 56.
5. Brueggemann, *Creative Word*, 12.

of the community. Through Ecclesiastes, the unknowable character of Yahweh is experienced alongside the tangible creation that mirrors his qualities and the profound correlation between the created and cohesive plans of the Creator. Finally, Song of Songs intensely illustrates how the unimaginable becomes real through the imagery that both surprises and lures the readers to learn experientially through the senses. Throughout Wisdom Literature, active learning is powerfully portrayed through multiple means of engaging the learner to listen, observe, and participate as the religious ethos is transferred from one generation to the next.

Chapter 1

Active Learning

ACTIVE LEARNING CAN BE found within the confines of any community including families, organizations, and institutions. Humanity is composed of many different sizes and types of social communities that construct their own ethos and mythos based on their experiences and traditions. These communities typically share a geographical location, common beliefs, occupations, or other similar interest. Important aspects or characteristics of the group are transferred from elder generations to younger generations within the families or other organizations within the community. If a community is to succeed, it must concern itself with education. A great deal of information is passed on though the educational process, both formally and informally, promoting the growth and substance of the community. This information includes history, social and cultural norms including values and beliefs of the community. Its main objective is to prepare the younger generation for its future responsibilities. This includes expected skills, information, and standard rules of conduct. A historical and global look at the topic reveals that education has been used to convey ideas of governance, health, moral values and religious ideals.[1]

FORMAL AND INFORMAL EDUCATION

The value of education remains uncontested in most countries. In recent years, ongoing studies continue to build the body of knowledge on the

---

1. Hagglund, et al. "Early Childhood Education," 49–63.

best methods for educating both adults and children. Education is intrinsically integrating in many aspects of daily living. At its core, education is the transmission of knowledge, ethics, and worldview from one person to another. Though education continues to develop and adapt throughout history and cultural environments, its fundamental premise remains unchanged. Education involves the entire process by which accumulated knowledge, social norms, and religious ideals are transmitted from one generation to the next in each society.

While education is the product of the direct action of teachers, there is a distinction between formal and informal education. Formal education is "conventional, given in an orderly, logical, planned, and systematic manner."[2] Typically, this formal type of education takes place in a classroom, or other formal setting. The information in this setting is similar across the classroom, regardless of culture, gender, race, or socioeconomic status of the learner. While the teacher may attempt to address various learning styles, the learning objectives are typically the same. The resources available to the teacher may impact the instruction, but the teacher strives to teach the same lesson content to all learners.

In contrast, informal education occurs through the daily interactions that take place through shared experiences. Participation in social activities provides the learner informal education in areas such as social expectations, cultural heritage, and religious practices.[3] Similarly, N.L. Gage and David Berliner define learning as "the process whereby [a learner] changes its behavior as a result of experience."[4] They go on to state, "learning is what we infer has taken place when the behavior [...] has changed."[5] These experiences, however, may be dependent on socioeconomic status and resources available. Arguably, children from a more affluent family or community would have opportunities not available to children of a lower socioeconomic status.[6] Certain cultural tools may vary based on the learner's community and environment. Arguably so, enhanced childhood experiences are not necessarily limited to income. Included in the both the formal and informal aspects of education, is religious instruction. Beliefs and values can be taught in formal settings

---

2. Good, *Dictionary of Education*, 175.
3. Pazimiño, *Foundational Issues*, 84.
4. Gage and Berliner, *Educational Psychology*, 252.
5. Ibid.
6. Fleer, "Cultural Construction," 127–40.

such as a religious gathering as well as informally through family and peer groups. For the purpose of this study, the focus remains centered on informal religious instruction.

IMAGINATION IN LEARNING

Education calls on the imaginations of both the instructor and the learner. Imagination has long been associated with role play which is a natural occurrence in childhood. Through play, children practice and process new ideas and address frustrations in a safe environment. Winnicott claims, "In playing, and perhaps only in playing, the child or adult is free to be creative."[7] Dewey explains that this imagination, or play, allows experiences to be reshaped and create possibilities that do not exists in mere reality. Through this process, reality can be made to make some sort of sense. Even in adulthood, by considering a person's imagination, it is easy to spot the frustrations that exist in their reality. This use of imagination allows humans to play, problem solve, and create, thereby producing a means for learning through imagination.

Within education, imagination, play, and learning can occur in many ways. This text will consider two ways. Education occurs as the teacher takes on the role of teaching directly to the learners or as a facilitator, creating situations and space where imagination and learning can occur. In direct teaching, the instructor creates an environment conducive to learning and determines the information to be transmitted to the learner. Lessons typically take place in an oral format. The learner's responsibility lies in consuming the information, linking it to prior knowledge, and memory for future use. When the teacher takes on the role as a facilitator of learning, however, learning activities and inquiry replace the focus on oral instruction. Simply stated, education depends, in part, upon the philosophy of the instructor. In an environment, such as Dewey describes, education surpasses the boundaries of the information presented and becomes a place of inquiry where authentic learning can take place. Children learn from both physical experiences and imagined reality.

Educational philosophy varies greatly among educators. Many prefer to think in terms of extreme opposites. It is given to formulating its beliefs in terms of polarized choices, between which it recognizes no

---

7. Winnicott, *Playing and Reality*, 53–54.

intermediate possibilities. When forced to recognize that the extremes cannot be acted upon, it is still inclined to hold that all choices are correct. Educational philosophy is no exception.[8] Relativism or absolutism are two pedological techniques discussed in detail by scholars. While some scholars hold fast to one extreme or the other, consideration for a middle ground has also been discussed. Scholars such as Jennifer Bleazby correctly argue that neither philosophy is appropriate when working with children and suggests a compromise, or middle ground, that can be found in the work of John Dewey, Lorraine Code, and Sandra Harding.

Bleazby maintains that neither relativism and absolutism are appropriate in the area of pedagogy. Absolutism, Bleazby explains, typically refers to universal truths. Bleazby further explains that absolutism implies that there is "some universal culturally neutral pedagogy and curriculum that is equally suitable for all learners. In actuality, educational practices and standards usually reflect the interest and values of the dominant culture, while failing to account for various cultural, gender and racial difference in learning and thinking styles and values."[9]

There are other concerns regarding absolutism. Within the concept of absolutism and teaching, the instructor is the center of the educational process. The teacher is the ultimate authority of knowledge. Also, known as the "banking concept of schooling,"[10] the teacher makes deposits of knowledge into the minds of learners. Learners take on a more passive approach while the teaching determines what is both taught and learned. This philosophy for passive learning leaves limited opportunities for learners to engage in the learning process, and the learner becomes a container for whatever the teacher deposits.

Relativism, though problematic, is another option considered in the field of education. Bleazby explains that relativism is also an inappropriate choice. Relativism is "truth is constructed and relative to particular cultures, times, places or individuals."[11] There are several issues to consider regarding relativism. Based on the idea of this theory, truth is based on the perspective, beliefs, opinions, and values of both the teacher and learner. Since each of these are based on past experiences and no two people share identical experiences, relativism itself is subjective.

---

8. Dewey, *Experience and Education*, 17.
9. Bleazby, "Overcoming Relativism and Absolutism," 458.
10. Ibid., 454.
11. Ibid., 455.

Furthermore, Bleazby contends that "subjectivism is the narrowest form of relativism."[12] Truth is constructed and the individual constructing it cannot objectively look at the world void of feelings and opinions. Furthermore, this type of truth would again, vary from one person to the next since feelings and opinions are not universal. Additionally, if truth is based on one's perception and relativism is promoted as part of education, what is the outcome of truth constructed from faulty information? The assumption is that experiences promote growth and development within the person. Active, experiential learning then becomes the focus. Instructor initiated contexts allow learners to experience learned truth first hand. This is discussed in greater detail later in this chapter.

Created for Learning: Mirror Neurons

Evidence exists to explain the brain's propensity for learning. Much research has been and continues to be done to support this evidence. The human brain is a multifaceted structure with many interconnected pieces.[13] The lower parts of the brain, including the brain stem, deal with basic functions of the body. Temperature, respiration, heart rate and fight or flight survival responses are regulated from this region. The upper parts of the brain are used for thinking, reasoning, and problem solving. In the central part of the brain is the limbic system. This area coordinates the activities between the lower and upper regions and is instrumental in the processing of memory. As a whole, the brain works together for the learning process to take place by taking in, making sense of, storing, and retrieving information.

"The sensory, motor, and cerebral systems are essential tools used by humans to complete tasks, create goals, and add meaning to their lives."[14] The brain was created for the learning process from the beginning. The early discovery of mirror neurons in the brains of monkeys led to further research concerning humans. Research suggests that learning can take place through use of mirror neurons located the brain. Mirror neurons are a distinct kind of neurons that fire both when a human performs a motor activity and when the individual observes the exact or similar action. When eye-tracking measures were used, it was discovered that

---

12. Ibid., 455.
13. Siegel, *The Developing Mind*, 10.
14. Bandura, "Social Cognitive Theory," 22.

in humans, mirror neurons develop before the age of 12 months.[15] These findings suggest that learning begins taking place at a very early age.

It has long been determined that learning from observing is an effective model for humans.[16] Children observe and mimic behaviors of their siblings and parent. Early behaviors are often observed and repeated, not only in childhood, but also influence behaviors forming habits throughout one's life. Cognitive load theory (CLT) postulates that the way human thinking is organized makes imitating or learning by observation, an efficient way of learning instead of trying to obtain the all knowledge by personal experience.[17] Furthermore, studies recognize the brain's similar response to both real or imagined experiences. In this case, the learner can learn from both.

LEARNING THEORIES

Highly supported in the field of education is the role of active learning. Active learning emphasizes the learners' examination of values and learning through sensory experiences. When a learner (regardless of age) combines sight, touch, or smell with auditory instruction, the impact and memory retention far exceeds information retained through oral instruction alone. Active (experiential) learning is achieved when the learner participates through touch, activity, or inquiry. It is differentiated from passive learning where learners receive audible instruction with no involvement in the learning environment. In other words, a learner must experience the content through multiple senses to achieve maximum impact and memory retention. In reference to active/experiential learning, Tara Fenwick proposes that learners reflect on concrete experiences and/or participate in a community of practice by which they reflect on their experience.[18] Here, the focus is on the learner's ability to correlate meaning or new knowledge from the experience. Learning is embedded in the experience through which the learner participates. The outcome of experiential learning through participation in community practices is that the learner, "refines its practices, develops new ones, or discards

---

15. Acharya and Shukla, "Mirror Neurons," 118–24.
16. Bandura, *Social Foundations*.
17. Van Gog, et al., "The Mirror Neuron System," 1:21–30.
18. Fenwick, *Learning Through Experience*, 22.

and changes practices that are harmful or dysfunctional."[19] Furthermore, learners "[seek] to transform existing social orders, by critically questioning and resisting dominant norms of experience."[20]

Prior to Fenwick's study, considerable support for the value of experiential learning is well documented. John Dewey strongly concludes, "all genuine education comes about through experience."[21] Likewise, Peter Jarvis states, "all learning begins with experience."[22] Both David Kolb and Malcolm Knowles advocate the significance experiential learning. Kolb contends, "Learning is a continuous process grounded in experience. Knowledge is continuously derived and tested out in the experience of the learner."[23] It is through experiences that learners process and assimilate information. New experiences are instinctively compared to former experiences. Similarly, the outcomes of these experiences are considered, by the learner, and decisions are made based on whether the learner concludes the outcome has a positive or negative effect. It is through experience (or active learning that is combining multiple senses) that the maximum impact and memory retention is achieved. However, not every experience produces an acquisition of new knowledge. For experiential learning to occur, Dewey argues that two principles must occur. First, "the principle of the continuity of experiences means that every experience both takes up something from those which have gone before and modifies in some way the quality of those which come after."[24] Merriam, Caffarella, and Baumgartner agree with Dewey as they clarify his conclusion, "In other words, experiences that provide learning are never just isolated events in time. Rather, learners must connect what they have learned from current experiences to those in the past as well as see possible future implications."[25] Dewey's second principle, interaction, suggests an experience results in learning because of a transaction between the individual and the learning environment.[26] The atmosphere or learning context must provide the link between observation and necessity of new information.

19. Ibid., 27.
20. Ibid., 38.
21. Dewey, *Experience and Education*, 13.
22. Jarvis, *Twentieth Century Thinkers*, 16.
23. Kolb, *Experiential Learning*, 27.
24. Dewey, *Experience and Education*, 27.
25. Merriam, et al., "Experience and Learning," 2.
26. Dewey, *Experience and Education*, 41.

While Dewey (1938) explored how people learned from life experiences, Kolb and Kolb (2005) went one step further. They examined the works of John Dewey, Jean Piaget, Carl Jung and Carl Rogers, among others, and they compiled six general propositions of experiential learning theory. First, 'learning is best conceived as a process, not in terms of outcomes' (p. 194). Second, 'learning is relearning' (p. 194). Student's ideas must be drawn out, discussed, and refined. Next, learning requires a resolution of 'dialectically opposed modes of adaptation to the world;" that is, learners must move between 'opposing modes of reflection and action and feeling and thinking' (p. 194). Fourth, learning is holistic. Fifth, learning involves interactions between the learner and the environment. Last, learning is constructivist in nature.[27]

For Kolb, the learner oscillates between the concrete experience and reflective observation to active experimentation. Behavior patterns are learned through the observation of others and experimentation with one's own experiences. Bryant, Johnston, and Usher build on Kolb's writing as they insert that the experience itself is interpreted by the learner with no final definitive meaning. Instead the experience remains open to reinterpretation.[28] Later experiences may impact, reinforce, or alter the interpretation of an earlier experience.

Within education, is the *means* by which this knowledge is transmitted, also known as pedagogical theory. Peter Mortimore defines pedagogy as, "any conscience activity by one person designed to enhance learning in another."[29] Pedagogy is the instructional method or strategy for teaching. It is the process utilized by educators for transmitting information from one person to another. Pedagogy specifically refers to the instruction to children. The term andragogy refers to the instruction to adults. It was introduced by Alexander Kapp and 1883 and later popularized by Malcom Knowles.[30] While modern scholars in education continue to highlight the distinct learning differences between children and adults, pedagogy continues to refer to the entire context of instruction and may be used universally when referring to the education for both child and adult learners. Pedagogy reflects the full spectrum of instruction such as:

27. Merriam, et al., "Experience and Learning," 3.
28. Bryant, et al., *Adult Education*, 104–5.
29. Mortimore, *Understanding Pedagogy*, 17.
30. Knowles, *The Modern Practices of Adult Education*.

environment for instruction, learning format, and relationship between the instructor and learner. The learning format is more popularly classified as learning style. Adrian Furnham defines learning style as, "the composite of characteristic cognitive, affective, and psychological factors that serve as relatively stable indicators of how a learner perceives, interacts with, and response to the learning environment."[31] These learning styles and the efficiency of their counterpart, learning theories, is highly debated and criticized between scholars in education and psychology.

The incorporation of learning theories contributes several advantages when making an allowance for how people learn. One advantage is gaining insight into the characteristics that motivate human learning. This insight can then be used to create a learning environment and instructional approach that produces the greatest impact on learning and memory retention.[32] The conceptual framework for active learning includes an emphasis on learner interaction or participation through sensory experiences. Learning theorists such as Howard Gardner and Neil Fleming advocate that people learn in a variety of ways. Most often, a person favors one learning style over another. Gardner's theory of "Multiple Intelligences" was introduced in 1983, describing six main ways in which people learn and retain information. Gardner defines an intelligence as a set of problem-solving skills that enables an individual to resolve the assimilation of new information he or she encounters thereby allowing the learner to acquire new knowledge.[33] According to Gardner, and intelligence is an intrinsic means by which one learns. Like Gardner, Neil Fleming advocates that learning often occurs in a single or combination of intrinsic modes such as visual, aural, reading–writing, and kinesthetic learning.

Visual learning (Fleming), or spatial intelligence (Gardner), occurs when information is taken in through observation of an object or actions that can be visibly seen in the eyes. Aural (Fleming), or linguistic intelligence (Gardner), occurs through verbal communication and audible instruction. Kinesthetic learning (Fleming) occurs through physical activity. Rather than watching a demonstration, kinesthetic learners prefer to internalize information their active involvement or personal physical modeling. Gardner refers to kinesthetic learning as bodily—kinesthetic

---

31. Furnham, *The Psychology of Behaviour*, 189.
32. Ormrod, *Human Learning*, 7.
33. Gardner, *Frames of Mind*, 160–61.

intelligence. Both Fleming and Gardner refer to reading as a form of learning or intelligence. Since this category is addressed through the written record of the Hebrew Bible, the discussions within this study will remain focused on visual, aural, and kinesthetic learning styles.

Similar to Gardner and Fleming, Peter Jarvis advocates the importance of experiential learning. He further theorizes that learning occurs through the five senses of sound, sight, smell, taste, and touch. For Jarvis, learning is ultimately dependent on these senses throughout the learning process.[34] As previously asserted, not every experience results in learning. Under Jarvis' theory, learning only occurs when the learner cannot accommodate or assimilate a present experience with existing knowledge from prior experiences. This creates a disequilibrium, or inability to solve a problem. This imbalance and unease triggers learning. On the contrary, if the individual chooses to ignore the disequilibrium, then no learning occurs.[35] Prior to Jarvis, Jean Piaget argued that learners seek to maintain an intellectual balance (equilibration). According to Piaget, learners use equilibration for stability and coherence in order to comprehend inconsistencies in experience. Equilibration is the natural propensity to balance the content one already knows with new experiences. Likewise, learners use patterns in order interpret new experiences. These new experiences are then assimilated or accommodated. Assimilation occurs when the new experiences fits with the learner's comprehension from previous experiences whereas accommodation occurs when a new experiences requiring the learner to change an existing understanding to incorporate the new experience; in other words, the new information does not fit the pattern of the existing information.[36] When the equilibration balance is disrupted from new information not fitting the previously established patterns of information attained by the learner, it causes disequilibrium.[37]

While other learning theorists discuss their studies of learning styles, Gardner insists his notion of "multiple intelligences" is not synonymous with "learning styles." This is largely reflective of his definition and use of the term "style." According to Gardner, a learning style is a hypothesis of how one approaches a range of material. However, he views this as incoherent with no persuasive evidence. For example, when examining

---

34. Jarvis and Parker, *Human Learning*, 13.
35. Merriam, et al., "Knowles's Andragogy," 10.
36. Biehler and Snowman, *Psychology Applied to Teaching*, 58.
37. Yount, *Created to Learn*, 77.

auditory learning, Gardner notes that both speaking and music activate the ears yet access two different cognitive abilities. Recognizing this, Gardner promotes his theory of intelligences because it focuses on how an individual acts upon the sensory information and not the sensory function itself.[38]

There is a strong correlation between Flemming's and Gardner's research and both are well supported by other scholars in their field. Howard Gardner's research remains ongoing as he seeks to document whether there are additional intelligences that should be identified and included. He has developed a strong rubric for determining what constitutes an intelligence. Both theorists are well respected. Therefore, I have elected to use Fleming's terminology for two reasons. First, he is consistent in his use of four categories (visual, aural, reading, and kinesthetic) while Gardner continues to maintain the potential of additional intelligences. I am however, interested in his final conclusions for the religious intelligence and how this could impact future studies. My second reason for using Fleming's terminology is its simplicity. There are several aspects of this study that complicate its message. I therefore advocate incorporating simple structures, where possible, to facilitate clearer lines of communication.

Social Cognitive Approach

One of the dominant learning models observed in Wisdom Literature is through the interaction of the learner with the faith community and social structures described within the Hebrew Bible. Within the field of psychology, this is referred to as social cognitive theory. As a developing theory within social psychology, there remains little consensus on the mental constructs within close social relationships.[39]

Lev Semyonovich Vygotsky asserts the role of culture, society, languages and interaction are important components for understanding classifying how humans learn. In addition, Vygotsky argues that cognitive development comes from social interactions rather than being based on developmental stages as others suggest. "We already know that the child's chronological age cannot serve as a reliable criterion for establishing

---

38. Strauss, "Howard Gardner."
39. Fletcher and Fitness, *Knowledge Structures*, 3.

the actual level of his [sic] development.⁴⁰" Assuming knowledge is established through culture, Vygotsky studied learning in children from a socio-cultural approach. He describes his approach as "cooperative" and "cultural." He further asserts that thoughts, language, and reasoning is developed as a direct result of culture through social interactions. Therefore, these abilities represent the shared knowledge of a particular cultural community.[41] Furthermore, Vygotsky argues that child development is revolutionary as opposed to evolutionary.[42] The teacher projects learning out beyond the child's current capabilities creating opportunities to connect culturally, socially, and educationally. The child will reach beyond the current capabilities and find sense and meaning in the new learning.

The social cognitive approach is based on the principle that ideas relevant to awareness and understanding of information are fundamental to understanding all human responses that are both social and nonsocial in nature.[43] Social learning theory is fundamental for assessing the role of teaching paradigms. Robert Wyler asserts, at its core, thinking involves acting on and reacting to a world that is primarily social in nature.[44] The foremost motivation in building relationships centers on two main goals. The first goal is epistemic, or a desire to know the origin of truth of people. The second goal is relationship and self-enhancement. There is considerable argument that suggests people use human relationships to better understand one's self.[45] Jeanne Omrade concludes, "[the] social cognitive theory focuses on what and how people learn from one another, encompassing such concepts as observational learning, imitation, and modeling."[46] The study of learning through imitation was initiated through the 1941 book by behaviorists Neal Miller and John Dollard and later popularized in the early 1960's.[47]

Social interaction is an important means by which children learn the nuances of their culture. Parents, adults, and peers fulfill a vital role

40. Vygotsky, "Pedagogy of the Adolescent," 99.
41. Li and Lam, "Cooperative Learning," 2.
42. Vygotsky, "Pedagogy of the Adolescent," 31–184.
43. Wyler, et al., *Handbook of Social Cognition*, ix.
44. Ibid., x.
45. Fletcher and Fitness, *Knowledge*, 4.
46. Ormrod, *Human Learning*, 118.
47. Ibid.

in the learning process through the modeling of behavior as well as direct instruction and feedback. Modeling and oral instruction becomes active learning (rather than passive learning) when the learner has the ability to inquire of the significance of a behavior or instructions. Questions and answers become interactive between the teacher and the learner thus signifying active learning. Learners likewise use conversations when working with peers to reach decisions or communicate personal belief or understanding of previously acquired information. As they exchange ideas, and information passes between them, they generate and develop knowledge through the appropriation of their social context and environment. Learning is then achieved by the active participation of the learners within the social constructs of their social community. Activity is an important component for learning as is a key component in the social cognitive approach.[48] This is likewise supported in Acharya and Shuklas' discussion of mirror neurons.[49]

Like Omrade, Gage and Berliner assert learning is motivated through social constructs and behavior is acquired by observing the reward and/or punishment associated with an observed behavior.[50] Moreover, social learning acknowledges the fundamental importance of vicarious reinforcement for behavior and that learning consistently occurs while watching the positive or negative reinforcement of behavior for a different individual than oneself. For example, if a sibling is verbally praised or rewarded for exhibiting a desired behavior, a different sibling learns as much as if he or she were the one personally rewarded for the behavior.[51] Studies repeatedly support that people learn through modeled behavior. When an action is witnessed by an observant learner, the action is retained. Later, the learner can reproduce the action. The negative or positive reinforcement has a powerful effect on future behavior. Both direct and vicarious reinforcement have similar long-term effects on the memory retention and whether or not the newly learned behavior is repeated.[52]

As observed in Wisdom Literature, informal education occurs in the social context of life experience. Control of individual actions is affected

---

48. Li and Lam, "Cooperative Learning," 3.
49. Acharya and Shukla, "Mirror Neurons," 118–24.
50. Gage ad Berliner, *Educational Psychology*, 340.
51. Ibid., 341.
52. Ibid., 348.

by the whole context or situation in which multiple individuals are involved and share in the co-operative experience. John Dewey illustrates this concept through the analogy of team sports. These games involve rules which order the contact of the players. The players' actions are not haphazard or created through improvisation. Instead they are systematically reinforced through the rules of the game. In fact, the game ceases to exist without rules. If there is a dispute between players, an umpire or referee arbitrates and reaches a decision. The players do not feel subjected to the personal will of the game's creator nor controlled by the rules of the game. Rather, they maintain the rules of the game established through tradition and precedent.[53] In the same way in which players coordinate their actions by engaging the rules of the games, so people coordinate their actions by engaging the parameters defined by their social context. It is through the well-established expectations of the social community that mutual confidence is derived. Sociability and community are not created spontaneously or haphazardly. Instead, "rules for engagement" are formulated through tradition and precedent.

Social cognitive theory suggests learning occurs through the modeling and imitation of expected behaviors. Awareness and responsibility as well as reward and punishment are essential components of the learning process.[54] Here, new behaviors are learned through the observation of others' actions and the consequential reward or punishment that follows the action. This positive and negative reinforcement is a critical factor to the learning process.[55] Individuals learn new behaviors through the observation of others. This may be reinforced through audible instructions that either accompanies of follows the modeled behavior. For example, a child learns to swing a bat by watching how a parent swings a bat followed by verbal instructions for hand placement and muscle coordination.[56]

Behavior is not learned solely through trial and error and consequently modifying one's own behavior based on the outcome. Social cognitive theory proposes that not only do individuals learn through their own actions, but they learn through the observation of the actions of others. Most importantly, individuals learn through observing the outcomes

---

53. Dewey, *Experience and Education*, 52–53.
54. Ormrod, *Human Learning*, 119.
55. Ibid.
56. Ibid., 127.

from those behaviors.[57] Likewise, Dewey points out, observation alone does not produce learning. The learner must connect significance with what he or she sees, hears, or touches. The significance of the observation is derived from the consequences that result from personal action or observed action. He illustrates this by a child's natural attraction to a candle's flame. The significance of the flame is not its brightness but the burn that occurs when he or she reaches to touch it. Thus, learning occurs through the consequence of the action.[58]

> We can be aware of consequences only because of previous experiences. In cases that are familiar because of many prior experiences we do not have to stop to remember just what those experiences were. A flame comes to signify light and heat without our having expressly to think of previous experiences of heat and burning. But in unfamiliar cases, we cannot tell just what the consequences of observed conditions will be unless we go over past experiences in our mind, unless we reflect upon them and by seeing what is similar in them to those no present, go on to form a judgment of what may be expected in the present situation.[59]

Dewey summarizes the complexity of formulating significance through three factors: (1) observation of actions, (2) knowledge of similar situations through either personal experience or the testimony of the experiences of others, (3) judgment which combines observation with what it signifies.[60]

HOW MODELING AFFECTS BEHAVIOR

Humans are more likely to perform behaviors that they observe. When witnessing behaviors, the observer makes note of when behaviors are reinforced. Humans will most likely perform actions for which they are rewarded and avoid those behaviors that are punished. In effect, observers find that vicarious punishment is an incentive to avoid the punished behaviors.[61] Sometimes, however, behaviors that have been modeled and

---

57. Ibid., 119.
58. Dewey, *Experience and Education*, 68.
59. Ibid., 79–80.
60. Ibid., 68.
61. Ormrod, *Human Learning*, 127.

determined to be forbidden are repeated by the observer regardless of the outcome. If the observed individual is rewarded for performing the forbidden behavior, the observer is more likely to repeat the behavior. Henceforth, the forbidden behavior is rewarded creating vicarious reinforcement for the observer. This vicarious reinforcement has a "disinhibition effect."[62]

Because observation is the first critical step in social cognitive learning, the ability of the learner to notice the modeled behavior is a crucial component of the process. Furthermore, the degree to which the learner focuses his or her attention contributes to the propensity to commit the action to memory. The second stage in learning through modeled behavior is memory retention. Once a learner notices a behavior, it must be committed to memory for it to be later imitated. Biehler and Snowman suggest the memory may solely include the behavior itself or may encompass the behavior as well as its rationale.[63] Third, the modeled behavior must be reproduced or imitated. Finally, the behavior must be reinforced. As previously stated, this reinforcement may take place directly (affecting the learner himself) or vicariously (affecting someone else with a similar behavior). Both direct and vicarious reinforcement produce similar affects for memory retention and determining whether the behavior is repeated based on the negative or positive reinforcement.[64] As previous stated, the brain has a propensity for learning. Mirror neurons support the likelihood or possibility that an observed behavior will be repeated. Since humans not only use mirror neurons to encode the action being observed, but its details, and how action is performed making imitation a natural part of learning.

Children appear to acquire moral behaviors partly through observation and modeling.[65] Often these behaviors are mimicked in the form of play and can also be spotted when observing their interactions with other children. Information regarding acceptable and unacceptable behaviors are observed which enhances the children's ability to learn many things more quickly rather than having to experience all things one at a time.

---

62. Ibid.
63. Biehler and Snowman, *Psychology Applied to Teaching*, 314.
64. Ibid.
65. Ormrod, *Human Learning*, 131.

PEDAGOGY OF THE HEBREW BIBLE

Moloney advocates that the Hebrew Bible instructs its readers and listeners how to acquire knowledge. "Its pedagogy of social transformation instructs contemporary Christians how to interpret and apply lessons from Scripture in a manner that is consistent with the orientation, priorities and methods inherent in the text.[66]" Moloney explains that the forerunners to education are found first in relationship and identity. Knowing first and foremost that God is the Divine Teacher who "undertakes a continuous and integrated plan of holistic education with a set purpose and process.[67]" Furthermore, the Hebrew Bible holds page after page of recorded relationships with humankind and the Divine Teacher creating the first recorded form of active learning.

Following this same thought, within the contents of active learning is the identity and relationship of the teacher and the learner. The teacher attempts to engage the learner in the learning process by using the using the senses. The relationship from "knowing, trust, respect and mutuality—create a transformative space in which students are affirmed, gain insight into their potential, and grow toward fulfilling personal and professional capacities: student–teacher connection emerges as a place of possibility."[68]

Within the Hebrew Bible, and specifically Wisdom Literature, writers take it upon themselves to record their ethos and mythos. Alongside these accounts, they also record their means, or pedagogy, in which informal religious education occurred. As the next several chapters will show, the writers of the Wisdom texts advocate active learning through a combination of observations of nature and observations of members of the community. The examples that follow will show a direct correlation of Neil Fleming's VARK learning theory as well as social cognitive learning theory. In addition, there are strong examples of learning through senses as discussed by Peter Jarvis and learning through imagination and role play as promoted by John Dewey.

---

66. Moloney, *Pedagogy of Social Transformation*, 1.

67. Ibid., 2.

68. Gillespie, *Student–Teacher Connection*, 211.

Chapter 2

A Literary Approach

The preceding chapter summarized some of the current research relating to education. The research presented in chapter 1 indicated that learners learn through a variety of means. It further concluded that scholars agree that active learning surpasses passive learning on affecting long-term memory retention. It also discussed the relationship between learning through personal physical experience as well as observation ad imagined experience. All three modes impact the learner's ability to respond and retain information.

As I continue to trace how adherents of Yahwistic faith were taught the fundamental principles of their religious beliefs, the ethos of Wisdom Literature must be examined for its value of religious training. Here, I will demonstrate how the final form of the Wisdom corpus includes descriptions of pedagogy similar to that established in the two preceding chapters of this thesis. This genre is included in my research because it is often the primary genre studied when examining teaching and learning as they relate to the recorded ideals of religious training in biblical literature. While the didactic nature of the Wisdom genre is emphasized by M.V. Fox,[1] and H. Gese,[2] the following chapters will examine specific examples of pedagogy recorded in Wisdom Literature. The relationship in the pedagogical function of each of the Wisdom texts will be examined and discussed. It would be presumptuous to attempt an exhaustive list of Wisdom texts that present forms of pedagogy. Instead, representative

1. Fox, "Ancient Near Eastern."
2. Gese, "Wisdom Literature in the Persian Period."

texts are selected from Job, Proverbs, Ecclesiastes, and Song of Songs to illustrate and support the premise that the pedagogy articulated within these books represent active and social cognitive learning. The selection of these sample texts is based on their examples of learning or instruction. That is, passages that describe or provide an example of pedagogy are reviewed, those containing specific descriptions are then selected for further examination and discussion within each of the following chapters.

Wisdom Literature addresses various characteristics of human existence, including religious instruction. Both Job and Ecclesiastes hold to prominent religious view of retributive theology. The theology of retribution finds its roots in the Pentateuch, namely Deut. 28. It maintains the perspective that good deeds are always rewarded by Yahweh and disobedience to his law leads to punishment. In support of this dichotomy is the book of Proverbs, which seemingly endorses and promotes this worldview with the collection of instruction on how to please God and succeed in life. Finally, the series of love poems collected in the Song of Songs also addresses various aspects of human life, including instruction.

WISDOM DEFINED

The word, "wisdom," expresses a range of meanings within biblical literature. On one hand, a wise man is someone who has achieved notable respect for the knowledge he processes in his artistry or trade. Specifically, as it applies to Wisdom Literature, a wise man is not someone who has merely acquired the knowledge of God's word. Instead, it is the person who can apply God's word and make the morally correct choice, even if it means one's own demise. Thus, those who know God's law and can appropriately apply it will succeed in life and are thus considered wise.

The writing style of Wisdom Literature is found in several countries including but not limited to Egypt, Mesopotamia, and Israel. It crosses over multiple genres such as proverbs, instruction, dialogue, poetry, and narrative. Michael Coogan argues that much of this literature consist of collections created by scribes under the control of various monarchy and originally available to the socially elite.[3] There is greater diversity in the collection of "Wisdom Literature" found outside the biblical Wisdom books. These writings bear distinct features of the various cultures.[4]

---

3. Coogan, *Brief Introduction*, 384.
4. Lucus, *Exploring*, 81.

Wisdom as Literature

Wisdom Literature is a style of writing that flourished throughout the ancient Near East from the third century B.C. to the first century A.D. with remarkable similarity in different countries and eras.[5] Although there are examples of Wisdom Literature throughout both the Hebrew and Greek canon, the majority of this genre is found in the collection, Writings. The feature of biblical wisdom that often receives the most attention in its applicability to routine, daily events.[6]

The Dead Sea Scrolls provided a framework for questioning the parameters for defining a text as "Wisdom." Prior to the availability of these scrolls, Wisdom Literature essentially included Ben Sira and the Wisdom of Solomon.[7] After the discovery of the Dead Sea Scrolls, conversations ensued over several extra-biblical texts such as 4QInstruction. However, despite the interest in Qumran wisdom texts, relatively little attention is attributed to Wisdom as a genre and identifying what it means to designate this writing style as a distinct composition.[8] Matthew Goff adequately addresses this issue in his 2010 publication where he supports his claim that the label of "Wisdom" is a legitimate genre category, though he admits the breadth of literature that could reasonably be attributed to this category. He further notes that this classification is not rigidly defined by the authors of this literature.[9]

The discovery of the Dead Sea Scrolls allowed for further study regarding the coherence of Wisdom as its own genre of literature. The Qumran wisdom texts led to Goff's definition of this literature as having "instructional purpose." He goes on to further define this as "literature written for the education of particular individuals who were supposed to strive for understanding."[10] Goff's definition affirms the definition established earlier by Hartmut Gese. Like Goff, Gese establishes Wisdom as a distinct genre of literature and defines it as biblical literature with an instructional purpose that is not part of the Pentateuch.

While both Goff and Gese agree on the didactic intentions of Wisdom Literature, neither one offers a definitive category that establishes a

---

5. Coogan, *Brief Introduction*, 383.
6. Berry, *Introduction to Wisdom*, 4.
7. Goff, "Qumran Wisdom Literature," 315.
8. Ibid., 316.
9. Ibid., 317–318.
10. Ibid., 326.

clear distinction between these texts and other literary genres. According to Gese's definition, prophetic texts such as Malachi may also be arbitrarily included for its didactic properties and exclusion from the Pentateuch. John Collins correctly speaks to this as he writes,

> While all sorts of material might conceivably be used for instruction, wisdom instructions can be distinguished from other genres, such as narrative, prophecy, law or hymnody. They may be cast in second-person direct address, whether hortatory or informative, or they can make use of third-person of putative fact. The coherence of Wisdom Literature, however, lies in its use as instructional material rather than in literary form, strictly defined.[11]

Like Goff and Gese, Collins emphasizes the instructional intent as the defining characteristic at the expense of attention to its form. While the instructional material and pedagogical function of these texts are key features of this literature, alone, they do not offer enough filter for limiting the texts to this specific genre. Recognizing this leads Goff to further stress, "Wisdom texts foster in their intended addressees a desire to search for understanding in the world."[12] In reference to the Qumran text, 4QInstruction, Goff correctly points out the clear emphasis within the Wisdom genre for the learner to pursue personal study and contemplation.[13]

At its core, Wisdom writing is an intentional perspective of rationally applying Yahweh's laws to everyday life. The religious perspectives portrayed in Wisdom Literature do not replace the theology found in the narrative and prophetic literature rather it complements those perspectives. Wisdom Literature initiates with the moral order described in the Torah. This is deeply illustrated in the book of Proverbs. The pursuit of knowledge included in the principles of the Torah leave Israel to seek a means for rationally applying its principles to the scope of life that extends beyond the concrete examples provided in the Torah. In its early stages, Israel views the Torah as the locus of wisdom. As they evolve in their relationship and worldview of Yahweh, they come to accept the idea of wisdom existing as a separate manifestation of understanding endowed

---

11. Collins, "Wisdom Reconsidered," 281.
12. Goff, "Qumran Wisdom Literature," 327.
13. Ibid.

by Yahweh.[14] "The adaptations and expansions of statements within Wisdom Literature in the Septuagint indicate that vitality of wisdom teaching during the development of the Septuagint."[15] The acceptance of Wisdom Literature as divinely inspired builds the importance of this genre's perspective, which is strikingly different from the narratives and prophets. Whereas other genres record the origins of humanity, relate the establishment of cultic rituals, and portray stories of founding figures and heroes, Wisdom Literature is dedicated to articulating a world with an informed sense of order grounded in retributive justice. Here, good and evil are contrasted as demonstrated in the two characters of lady wisdom and the adulterous woman in Proverbs. Characters do not blur both good and bad qualities such as those seen in the epic narratives of King David.[16]

Wisdom as Concept

The concept of wisdom is problematic. On more than one occasion, texts within the Wisdom corpus insist that the fear of the Lord is the beginning of wisdom. This concept of wisdom is espoused in Deut. 10:12 where covenant and respect are juxtaposed. Wisdom is the reasoned search for explicit descriptions of how to ensure daily success in one's life through social and political harmony.[17] According to the teachings of Proverbs, this harmony is achieved by diligent obedience to Yahweh's expectations communicated through His laws. Moshe Weinfeld suggests:

> Fearing God 'all the days' means constant awareness of God. No wonder, then, that the author of Deuteronomy exhorts the Israelites not to forget the Lord (6:12; 8:11, 14, 19). The causes of such forgetfulness are the pride and arrogance which come with material wealth and satiety (6:10–11; 8:12–13; 17:16–20; cf. 31:20; 32:13–15). The notion that affluence and satiety bring one to deny and forget God also belongs to wisdom ideology.[18]

The worldview integrated into this genre is evident through its sweeping panorama of recorded concepts such as: creation, justice, politics, and etiquette. This genre is also used to articulate the reconciliation

---

14. Berry, *Introduction to Wisdom*, 46.
15. Ibid., 51.
16. Alter, *Literary Guide*, 263.
17. Crenshaw, *Old Testament Wisdom*, 3.
18. Weinfeld, *Deuteronomy 1–11*, 280.

between the narrative accounts of Yahweh's justice and the realities experienced by the writers and/or audience of Wisdom Literature. The key to assimilating these two concepts is the fear of the Lord. For example, political order is preserved through the obedience of Yahweh's laws.[19]

In his book, *Wisdom in Israel*, Von Rad discusses the "understanding of reality" that is recorded within Wisdom Literature.[20] Here, the writers use the stories and traditions passed down to them through their ancestors to continue the emphasis of Yahweh's intervention in the lives of their current audience. Concrete examples of Yahweh's action are used to teach the religious ethos of the writers. Ronald Murphy agrees with Von Rad's analysis and goes on to state:

> The effective literary presentation of these views in pithy sayings tends to set them apart, without a concrete context to explicate them. But their original context was in history, and their further application is in the historical order. History is not merely the recollection of times past, but also the analysis of daily experience in which the variable and the incalculable often appear.[21]

Donald Berry introduces a basic definition of wisdom as "the exercise of mind as a religious pursuit."[22] While Berry's definition is broad, it adequately aligns with Goff's literary designation for Wisdom's instructional property and emphasis on personal contemplation therefore allowing the literary categorization of Wisdom and the concept of Wisdom to align. Berry further states, "What is appropriate in one context is out of place in another. The secret of wisdom is to know when and how. It involves the ability to match activities with the proper circumstances."[23] It is reasonable that James Crenshaw offers one of the clearest definitions when he states, "Wisdom is the reasoned search for specific ways to assure wellbeing and the implementation of those discoveries in daily existence. Wisdom addresses natural, human, and theological dimensions of reality, and constitutes an attitude toward life, a living tradition, and a literary corpus."[24]

---

19. Walton and Hill, *Old Testament Today*, 292.
20. von Rad, *Wisdom in Israel*, 6.
21. Murphy, *Tree of Life*, 113.
22. Berry, *Introduction*, 2.
23. Ibid., 3.
24. Crenshaw, *Wisdom*, 15.

The purpose of Wisdom Literature is to make sense of exasperating anomalies and to communicate elusive knowledge to successive generations. Wisdom itself seeks to logically apply the means for personal well-being. The ultimate goal is the formation of character.[25] The rationale for this instruction is for younger members of the community to learn to discern events according to the worldview of the elder members of their community.[26]

In general, the writers of the Hebrew Bible use the term wisdom (*hokmah*) to refer to both physical and intellectual skill. People who possess skill are described as "wise." However, this meaning narrows considerably within Proverbs, where *hokmah* always signifies appropriate living as the skill referenced.[27] "The Wisdom Literature is predicated on the assumption that wisdom can be acquired."[28] In Wisdom Literature, *hokmah* is often coupled with other words meaning knowledge or understanding and focuses on a more intellectual slant. It is also clear that wisdom is not the mere acquisition of information that rather how to live successfully through righteousness, justice, and moral fortitude; as noted in Prov. 1:5, this is a learned skill.[29] As such, the writers and editors also take special care to record how this skill is learned. The pedagogical features for passing this information from one individual to another are included in the Wisdom texts alongside the description of the skill.

The most prominent theme within Wisdom Literature is the theory of retribution. This principle is derived from the foundation of blessings and curses ascribed in Deuteronomy 28 as consequences of correct or incorrect behavior, in accordance with the prescribed law. The theory of retribution later developed as a means to relate how experiences reflected the writers' perceptions of Yahweh's action in sequence with man's behavior and obedience, or lack thereof, to his laws. Wisdom Literature describes good things happening as a result of Yahweh's reward for obedience. People experienced unfortunate consequences as a result of their negligence or direct disobedience to Yahweh's laws. As related in their literature, Israelites did not have a concept of reward and judgment in a life that followed a physical life on earth; therefore, these occurred in

---

25. Ibid., 3.
26. Brueggemann, *Introduction*, 308.
27. Whybray, *Proverbs*, 4.
28. Lucas, *Exploring*, 81.
29. Ibid.

their present lives as the result of Yahweh's justice. The Wisdom corpus vividly demonstrates a process concerned with building communities and social structures through a provided paradigm of values extracted from Yahweh's religious laws.

Rather than represent the actions of Yahweh, Wisdom Literature focuses on human experiences and the connection between Yahwism, wisdom, and blessings.[30] The overall use of active learning, specifically tangible imagery and social cognitive theory, is continuously utilized as the dominant pedagogy throughout the Wisdom corpus.

William Brown offers a proposal regarding the literary approach to Wisdom Literature. While attesting that the Wisdom genre is different than the Narrative genre, Brown acknowledges that narratives and Wisdom Literature share some characteristics. He defends that the final shape of Job is fundamentally a story using a basic setting, characters, plot, climax, and resolution. Likewise, the collection of wise sayings in Proverbs bare similarities to the "metanarrative" with an overall development that is not resolved until the final chapter.[31]

While Brown's analysis is intriguing, it is overtly simplistic and does not address the complexities of poetic imagery. Leo Perdue is more accurate in his assessment as he contends that assigning some of the texts of the Wisdom corpus to a single literary form fails to capture its literary nuances.[32]

To summarize, wisdom is a lens for viewing events that is informed by retributive justice.

> The sayings of the wise have been transmitted by the elders, who are to be held in respect, and this world-sustaining wisdom of the faith is maintained the individual and social discipline. Wisdom thus affirms a divine cosmic order and represent folly at disorder. It does not, however, impose a systematic view of order on the world and human behavior. Although human existence and the surrounding world are placed within the framework of order, individuals and situations are conceived of in the particularly and are not methodically organized into a system of abstractions.[33]

---

30. Murphy, *Tree of Life*, 1.
31. Brown, *Character*, 20.
32. Perdue, *Wisdom Literature*, 92.
33. Alter, *Literary Guide*, 265–66.

Wisdom Literature differs from the other genres within the Hebrew Bible. All genres presuppose a way for viewing the characteristics of the world. However, the perspective within Wisdom Literature is quite different from that of the narratives and prophetic literature. Whereas these genres seek to retell the establishment of the world, the nation of Israel, the religious traditions and the rise and fall of the monarchy, Wisdom Literature articulates a world ordered through the principle of retributive justice.[34]

Like the Hebrew narratives, Wisdom Literature uses the diverse qualities of its characters to portray an overall concept of religious expectations. Through these characters and the written texts, the final editors of the Wisdom corpus purposefully included examples of pedagogy for later generations to incorporate into their religious education.

LITERARY VERSUS HISTORICAL APPROACH TO INTERPRETATION

Literary, grammatical—historical, and theological interpretation are three popular approaches for biblical interpretation among contemporary scholars. All three methodologies offer unique contributions for exegesis and are valid approaches for interpretation of the biblical texts. It is also noted, that many interpreters use various combinations of these interpretive methods.

The grammatical historical method is the study of the biblical text in the original historical setting, seeking the meaning the author/editor most likely intended for the original audience. The interpretation is based on the grammar and composition of the biblical text. This method of interpretation affirms the feasibility of the historicity of the recorded accounts but does not conclude the historical factors are indisputable. Further, this interpretive method does not critique the historical accuracy of the text but rather interprets the text based on the record of historical accounts recorded in the text. Authorial intent is the determination of what the original writer most likely intended based on the information embedded in the text itself. It does not endorse intentional fallacy, whereby interpreters generate the mental actions/intentions of the writer. The grammatical-historical method encourages a textual meaning that is in line with what the original audience could have understood. The

---

34. Ibid., 263.

fuller meaning or foreshadowing represented in the biblical text moves beyond the role of grammatical-historical, which fundamentally uses only the original audiences' capacity of comprehension to determine meaning. Theological or literary analysis is more appropriately used to make conclusions of the text's *sensus plenior*.[35] In addition to the recorded accounts, this interpretive method accounts for the syntax of the biblical text. Because words have multiple meanings as well as distinct contextual meanings, the grammatical-historical method includes a careful analysis of the words, sentences, and composition of the text to determine the writer's flow-of-thought and base the interpretation on what makes sense within the context of the larger literary unit.[36]

Scripture is the vehicle used to provide readers with the knowledge needed to make informed decisions regarding behavior and the means for recognizing the source of salvation. The role of theological interpretation is to account for the development of theological underpinnings behind the stories collected, preserved, and recorded. In one lens, it accounts for why particular stories were necessary in the development of faith and justifies why writers likely chose to include the selected stories. In the second lens, theological interpretation explains the overall theological development of the current canon in its final form. Therefore, theological interpretation not only considers the development of Israel's faith and the stories amassed as their theological understanding developed, but it also considers the development of theological themes throughout scripture and how the stories continue to build off one another.

The literary approach for biblical interpretation is relatively new in its development. Pioneered by Erich Auerbach in 1947,[37] the literary approach directs attention to the text itself and its contextual connections and patterns. The literary approach addresses the purpose of the texts and the specific references to social and religious decorum as well as references to actions and geographical locations. While it is not indifferent to historical events, its focus remains on references embedded within the text itself. Rather than historical accuracy, it focuses on the plot and sequential action that propels the story forward. Likewise, narrators and characters drive the plot through its conflict, climax, and resolution. "This criticism is concerned with the text as a whole, its unity, the time

---

35. *Sensus plenior* is the Latin for "fuller meaning."
36. Bloomberg, "Historical," 27–39.
37. Bray, *Biblical Interpretation*, 467.

of its writing, questions about its author or authors, and the intentional changes that may be discovered in it."[38] The literary approach to biblical interpretation examines the role of the narrator and the purposeful details and descriptions included by the writers and/or inserted by later editors. It focuses on the rationale for these specific inclusions as clues for the intended meaning and focus of the text.

Because of the focus of textual nuances and specific attention on editorial activity regarding pedagogical features, the literary approach offers the best means for approaching the text and discussing these features within this study. This does not infer ambivalence to the historical value of the texts but rather a focus on the literary context for the inclusion of religious ideals described in connection with instruction. The literary approach selected for this study is a resource used to validate the presence of pedagogical features and determine their role within the biblical texts.

The literary context refers to the content surrounding a given passage and the knowledge that may be learned from its subject matter. The writers and editors of the Hebrew Bible use language and recorded literature as a means for training learners the religious ideals, moral instruction that construct their worldview. Intimately connected is the means, or pedagogy, by which instructions are communicated to these learners. The text itself becomes the medium to engage readers through the meticulously described actions and events surrounding characters who encompass or defend the ethos and mythos of the writers and editors.

AUTHORSHIP OF WISDOM LITERATURE

Likewise, biblical Wisdom Literature includes perspectives and literary pieces adapted from other cultures to construct its complicit instructions for interaction within the community. Kathleen O'Connor addresses an example of this adaption from the writings of Amen-em-opet and the striking similarities in Prov. 22:17—24:22. She goes on to discuss the broad inclusion of borrowed content from Egyptian, Sumerian, Akkadian, Babylonian, and Canaanite cultures.[39] The overtly didactic nature of Wisdom Literature is strongly presented throughout the collection of writings as well as its incorporation of adapted literature that is

---

38. Amit, *Reading*, 23.
39. O'Connor, *Wisdom Literature*, 23–24.

reconstructed to account for both the community expectations as well as the relevance to Israelite culture.

Wisdom is an "intellectual tradition"[40] passed from one generation to the next. The Israelite heritage of Wisdom Literature is the product of amassed collections of oral tradition and stories accumulating through shared knowledge. It is transmitted from the elder members of the community to the younger generations as a guide for correct conduct and resource for actively engaging in daily community life. The distilled experiences of the various members of the community become the collective identity of the nation. The transference of cultural experiences and stories from one nation to another are interwoven over time and adapted into the accepted collection of wisdom resources.[41] Later, these traditional sayings and repertoire of wisdom became the redacted writings of sages and the educated community who likely expanded the stories. James Crenshaw correctly states that wisdom writings were likely originally written by or for potential rulers with the intention of wider distribution.[42] He goes on to state that biblical Wisdom likely adopted the Near Eastern wisdom of knowledge mediating through tradition. "Just as vestiges of a magical view persisted for millennia, the old notion of a chain of tradition guaranteeing authentic teaching continued into the Common Era, specifically in the rabbinic tradition underlying the second-century mishnaic tractate *Pirke Aboth*."[43] Like biblical wisdom, non-Israelite wisdom texts focus on social relationships, speech, responsibility, and correct use of authority.[44] The similarities between biblical Wisdom and extra-biblical wisdom texts are striking. Scholars such as R.N. Whybray, James Crenshaw, and Claus Westermann offer expansive dialogs and conclusive support for the adaptive use of wisdom traditions into biblical Wisdom writings. The incorporation of non-Israelite literature into biblical Wisdom is nearly uncontested. Therefore, it will not be further discussed here. Instead, the focus resumes on the pedagogical features used within these texts and how they correlate with modern learning theories.

---

40. Whybray, *The Intellectual Tradition*.
41. O'Connor, *Wisdom Literature*, 32.
42. Crenshaw, *Old Testament Wisdom*, 2010, 6.
43. Ibid., 6
44. Ibid., 6

EDITORIAL ACTIVITY

Editorial Activity of the Hebrew Bible

While debates regarding minor adjustments for dates are ongoing, there are substantial studies regarding the editorial activity and canonization of the Hebrew Bible available. Settling the debate is not necessary for the support of this study. Therefore, except for a brief summary of existing studies, the argument for a specific date range is not included for authorship and editorial activity.

There is broad consensus for editorial activity and textual revisions for the Hebrew Canon. While dates remain disputed, Jack Lewis postulates, "[. . .] the collection of Law closed by 400 B.C.E., of Prophets closed by 200 B.C.E., and of Writings closed at the Council of Jamnia about 90 C.E."[45] It is fully acknowledged that these dates are widely challenged, as is the assembly of the Council of Jamnia itself. However, at minimum, these dates provide a framework for recognizing the relatively late period for finalizing the biblical texts.

The discretion of biblical editors allowed them to shape biblical texts based on their acceptance of inerrancy, historical validity, and hermeneutical methodology. This intentional and complex act of recording and shaping the biblical texts is the agent in which they express their religious ethos and mythos. The ongoing desire to preserve their traditions and religious ideals is an internal driver to assume the responsibility for assuring the reliability of the stories recorded, collected, and shaped. Acceptance of editorial activity need not challenge one's conviction of an inerrant and divinely inspired text. This conviction remains unaffected in recognizing the possibility of the inspiration process to not only cover the initial writing, but the editing, collection, and canonization of Scripture.[46]

The plenary verbal inspiration theory affirms the Holy Spirit guided the human writers through the writing process. As they select their own words, the writers are given freedom to express themselves based on their expertise and experience. Yet, the Holy Spirit interacts in such a way to ensure the words they select accurately communicate the meaning God intended. The plenary verbal inspiration upholds the authority and inerrancy of scripture while also recognizing the human element within the biblical texts. It efficiently addresses the biblical evidence for variations in

---

45. Lewis, "Jamnia Revisited," 149.
46. C.f. Plenary Verbal Inspiration.

writing and edited texts as it accounts for the entire writing, editing, and canonizing process as part of the inspired finished product that accurately reflects the divine message. The writers are permitted to incorporate stories familiar to them and reimagine them in such a way as to directly relate truth while affirming Yahweh as the ultimate author.

Editorial Activity of Wisdom Literature

Few scholars accept single authorship for any one of the books contained in the Wisdom corpus. Rather than discussing authorship, much discussion centers on the approximate time for the finalization of the editing process of each Wisdom book.

Job is typically identified as either an early text that is composed during nomadic period described in the Pentateuch or a later composition nearer to the Babylonian Exile. The earlier dating of this text is due to the internal suggestion of lifestyle that is similar to those described for the patriarchs in Genesis. Writers such as Alan Millard support this conclusion due to the literacy attained during this time.[47] Others conclude that the text of Job is a post-exilic work as supported by H.H. Rowley[48] and Tremper Longman, III.[49] I agree with Longman's conclusion that the early dating for the composition of Job is no longer widely held.[50] Longman also accurately reviews the leading ideas for the compositional history of Job and the various discussions of later additions and editorial phases, such as the suspected additions of Elihu's speeches or the editorial activity that reflects the change in Job's character from patient and accepting of his suffering to angry and challenging of Yahweh's justice.[51] Robert Alter arrives at a similar conclusion when he asserts that the poetry of Elihu's speeches are not aesthetically pleasing and thus point to a different author.[52] As a whole, Longman correctly emphasizes the unattainable proof that Job is the original authorial whole or editorial phases of composition. He also correctly identifies, "Determining a precise date

---

47. Millard, "The Question of Israelite Literacy," 22–31.
48. Rowley, *The Book of Job*, 21.
49. Longman, *Job*, 24.
50. Ibid.
51. Ibid., 25.
52. Alter, *The Wisdom Books*, 127.

for the final form of the books is not possible, nor is it important for interpretation."[53]

The composition of Proverbs is equally impossible to conclusively identify. While multiple authors are readily identified, the phases of compilation are not. Likewise, Ecclesiastes and Song of Songs share similar difficulties. Acknowledgement is given to the tradition of Solomonic authorship but this is readily dismissed due to ambiguity in this conclusion and inconsistency in the content and emphasis. Rather than earlier dates that would coincide with the reign of Solomon, there is much discussion that emphasizes a much later date, traditionally during the exilic period. Donald Berry makes an interesting assertion when he suggests,

> [. . .] the attribution of wisdom to court life came late the development of court history. The model for royal wisdom could have been adapted from the Assyrians or Babylonians and applied to Solomon retroactively. This would explain the lack of court sages and the lack of mention for court study of wisdom before Daniel. Perhaps for the entire population of Israel, emphasis on the formal study of wisdom came only in the exile.[54]

While Berry does identify the unlikelihood that Israel's commitment to wisdom instruction fell so far behind other civilizations, he also rightly declares, "The formative influence of the exilic and postexilic period must be recognized."[55] The Wisdom corpus shares a compilation tradition similar to that of the Pentateuch and Deuteronomistic History. That is, it is likely that portions of these texts are written and shared during earlier periods and receive their final form at a much later date. For example, it is certainly plausible that portions of Job are first told within the oral traditions of the faith community, later become written texts, and then receive the final formation and editing during the exilic period. While I adamantly agree with Longman's conclusion that the formation of these texts are unverifiable and thus improvable, the wide consensus is that the final form of each Wisdom book takes place at a later date, usually seventh century or later.

---

53. Longman, *Job*, 27.
54. Berry, *Introduction*, 38.
55. Ibid.

SUMMARY

The literary approach selected for this research allows for the examination of pedagogical features and the means by which they are emphasized within the biblical texts. The ethical ideals or ethos of the writers are represented in the characters and outcomes for actions that are recorded in Wisdom Literature. They include transparent character flaws, such as Job, as well as social conviction and expectations, as observable in the father figure portrayed Proverbs. These characters appeal to the readers as they mirror their own assumptions, suspicions, achievements, and failures. These characters learn through various modes for learning that are preserved within these texts as ongoing examples for pedagogy that reliably imparts religious obligations and assists the learner with encoding these ideals into long-term memory. Through these characters, as well as the role of the narrators, the hearers and readers learn vicariously through the successes and failures of the characters. As it will be presented in later chapters, a combination of active learning through Neil Flemings VARK learning theory and the social cognitive learning theory are consistently included within Wisdom Literature.

The main characteristic of the Hebrew Bible is its didactic role in communicating new generations of the faith traditions preserved within its texts. Therefore, it is incumbent on readers to focus on this communication and the body of knowledge contained therein. The following chapters will engage the discussion of the transmission of religious ethos through the conceptual framework of active learning models. Through the poetry and narratives of the Wisdom genre, the faith communities preserve and pass on their ideas. Included with these accounts are the pedagogical tools they used to better relate the intangible instructions with tangible means for committing these concepts to memory and further preserve the traditions. Therefore, along with their theology, the writers preserve their teaching techniques as primary tools for ongoing religious training. This precedent is further identified and discussed in the chapters that follow.

Chapter 3

Pedagogy and the Construction of Childhood

THE TWO PREVIOUS CHAPTERS discuss learning theories and the literary approach to scripture. These are used to begin the response to the research question, what type of pedagogical features are described in Wisdom Literature. The role of this chapter is to increase awareness and knowledge of the depiction of childhood described in the Hebrew Bible. As an emerging field in biblical research, there are few existing studies on this subject in comparison to the substantial studies in other social norms relating to biblical literature. In part, this is a result of relatively few biblical texts that directly describe the defining characteristics and roles of children. It is also, in part, due to a lack of interest until recent studies. It is also important to note that several of the existing studies discuss the role of children through a *non sequitur*[1] discussion that is influenced by Western perspectives. Because Wisdom Literature is didactic in nature with a focused audience on youth, it is important to gain competence in Israel's perspective on youth and their role within the culture. The content of this chapter is used throughout chapters 4–7 with respect to the descriptions of teaching as they relate directly to children.

The central focus of this chapter is the defining characteristics and roles of children that are described in the Hebrew Bible. The means for achieving this goal is an interdisciplinary approach through literary criticism of the biblical texts and reflection on some of the modern studies in construction of childhood to determine any interrelated content that

1. *Non sequitur* is Latin for "does not follow."

directly relates to the biblical context without compromising the content with Western influence. The importance and focus of the research remains on the biblical perspective of the child as observable within the final form of the Hebrew Bible.

This chapters fist seeks to define both child and childhood through the biblical conceptions of these terms. As a socially constructed perception, the biblical texts are examined to determine how the descriptions fit together to formulate more robust definitions of these terms. Children will then be discussed in the context of their roles within the biblical world. Again, the main source is the relatively few descriptions contained in the Hebrew Bible as well as using some of the existing studies that pertain to this subject. The chapter will end with a brief overview of the role of education for children as it relates to the periods depicted in Wisdom Literature. A distinction is made between formal and informal education with a specific focus on informal education as the means by which religious instructions were given. This becomes the foundation for the remaining research in chapters 4–7.

Universally, the development of childhood is thought to be based on observable behaviors and observable bodily changes that children go through at about the same age.[2] Hayes posits, "Childhood is both a biological reality and a social construct. It is defined not only by biology, but also by a particular society at a particular time in a particular way which represents the view that society has of childhood."[3] Smyth further explains the perception of childhood is both dependent on the context and time.[4] Furthermore, childhood as described in the biblical text is strikingly different than childhood described in modern Western studies.

Many factors influence the concept of childhood. These factors include social, economic, and political. These factors may vary depending upon the point in history they are discussed. It then, becomes necessary to set the stage for the conversation and create parameters for the discussion of childhood. Children in different parts of the world are valued differently. For instance, in the United States, families tend to be more child centered. "The child-centered family in the US manifests a particular softness towards children and tends to view childhood as an overly

---

2. Fleer, *Cultural Construction*, 129.
3. Hayes, "Children's Rights," 9
4. Smyth, *Concept of Childhood*, 161.

sentimentalized time in life [. . .]"[5] This view of childhood, to be certain, is much different than that of the Hebrew Bible. In the content that follows, focus will be given to defining childhood and the role of the child during biblical times.

DEFINING CHILDHOOD

There is a distinct semantic difference between child and childhood. As Keopf-Taylor points out, differentiating between these two terms is particularly useful in dismantling the tension and subjectivity in contributions toward these two research focuses.[6] "By specifying that 'childhood' refers to the social construction scholars are seeking to deconstruct and that 'children' refers to the living, physically immature individuals to whom such constructions have been applied, both goals not only become possible but can also feed each other."[7] In and of itself, childhood is culturally defined through personalized categories and trends each society recognizes as efficient markers of maturity. "In this way, it has become clear that at this time scholars cannot objectively study children; we can only study childhoods, the varying social constructions within which children function and adults relate to children and their own childhood memories."[8]

DEFINING THE BIBLICAL CHILD

Children are mentioned several times in the Hebrew Bible. Many of these passages refer to children as a precious or favored people, such as the children of Israel. These passages suggest that children are divinely important. Notably, children were expected to carry on the legacy of the family name. Other passages suggested that childhood was a place one should leave behind. "Childhood in itself was regarded as a stage of immaturity, ignorance, and deficient reason; therefore, education played a critical role in molding persons for adulthood."[9] Several verses explain the importance of teaching and disciplining children. Wherein it was

5. Steinberg, *World of the Child*, 127.
6. Keopf-Taylor, *Give Me Children*, 8.
7. Ibid.
8. Ibid., 11.
9. Carroll, "Children in the Bible," 121–34.

important that a child be well-trained and kept the family name in good standing.

One of the difficulties in examining the biblical conceptions of childhood is the lack of focus on this social sub-group. As Julie Faith Parker points out, the brief, passing references to children in the biblical text offer glimpses of the life of a child that are preserved within the stories.[10] Additionally, if it is accepted that childhood is a socially constructed perception, then it naturally follows that the conception of childhood of the biblical scholar likely differs from the conception of childhood within the biblical world. Even on the rare occasion when the age of a child is included in the biblical text, the socialization and psychological development of that character likely exceeds the perception of the reader. Furthermore, the classification of biblical childhood is further complicated by the characterization of the authors who themselves may possess a social construction of childhood that differs from the social context they create due to the "imaginative memory" and time that transpires between oral tradition and written narrative. "Children are ubiquitous in the Hebrew Bible both as characters and as figures of speech."[11] Berquist argues that the problem is even greater and that "biblical authors imagined childhood in ways that we cannot replicate in our own different culture but in ways that may well resonate with our own imaginings of childhood and adolescence."[12] Interestingly, more often ages are given for the aging rather than for children or adolescents. Berquist argues that the stages referred to by the authors do not necessarily reference to a particular age.

Within the boundaries of the biblical text, the developmental stage of "child" remains undefined. A specific age when a child moves to adult status is also unavailable. Furthermore, the boundaries of and roles of children are ambiguous at best, if not obsolete. Childhood slavery, the sale of children for debt payoff, and marital rights to young girls blur the patterns of what it means to be a child verses an adult within the Israelite communities described in the Hebrew Bible. While life stages are described, the biblical text is not specific about the stages nor are consistent ages included with the descriptions. Nevertheless, some distinctions are available regarding the life stages of children within the texts. Studies are

---

10. Parker, "You Are A Bible Child," 60.
11. Keopf-Taylor, *Give Me Children*, 22.
12. Berquist, *Childhood and Age in the Bible*, 523.

available with extensive discussions that include both biblical and extra-biblical support for stages ranging from infancy to geriatric.[13] The two classifications pertinent to this study are children and adults.

Infancy and early child development is identified as a suckling or a child that is yet to be weaned from his or her mother. This weaning typically occurred around three years of age.[14] The next major social distinction of classification is puberty. While it is accepted that the age for this classification likely varies among individual persons, the target range used here is 12–14 years old. Following puberty, most male and female children were married, thus distinctly classifying them within the social community as adults. However, the biblical text again suggests age variations for this life stage. Females married in their early teens while males may wait for the death of their father and the receipt of inheritance before becoming financially viable for marriage, thereby delaying the male's age of marriage considerably.[15] In summary, scholars have made fascinating contributions toward the reconstruction of life stages within the Israelite community. However, these do not reliably align with the texts of the Hebrew Bible. Furthermore, the biblical texts themselves do not offer consistent patterns of life stages for children and rites of passage for adulthood. Both internal and external evidence remains inconclusive.

Naomi Steinberg completed a relatively thorough analysis of the terms used for child in the Hebrew Bible[16] where she identifies that a lexical study on the term child insufficiently clarifies childhood in the biblical context.[17] Instead, she concludes that exegetical study, textual analysis, and cultural connotations are necessary components for identifying the biblical conception of childhood.[18]

For the purpose of this study, the terms referencing children that are of the most interest are those found in the context of teaching and learning. Examples include: Prov. 22:6, 29:5 נַעַר (na'ar), and Prov. 1:8 בֵּן (bên). Ben, occurring over 4,800 times in the Hebrew Bible is the most widely used term referring to children. It is most frequently used in reference to son or grandson, a male youth. When the term is used in combination

---

13. See Hans Wolff, *Anthropology of the Old Testament* and Karel van der Toorn, *From her Cradle to her Grave*.

14. Blenkinsopp, "The Family in First Temple Israel," 68.

15. Steinberg, *World of the Child*, 81.

16. Ibid., 26–41.

17. Ibid., 40.

18. Ibid., 41.

with the father's name, e.g. son of Jesse, it may refer to either a youth or adult male. When the term is used in combination with a location, e.g. sons of Israel, it refers to adult males. Though its plural use, without the combination of location, can refer to a mixture of both male and female children.[19] Na'ar is also commonly used, referring to an age range anywhere from newborn (Exod. 2:6) to a young man in his twenties (Gen. 34:19). Yet, its most prevalent usage pertains to adolescent young males.[20]

One of the most noteworthy scholarly contributions to the field of childhood studies in biblical literature is the 2014 publication by Kristine Garroway. In her study, Garroway surveys existing studies as well as examines both textual and archaeological evidence in both the Bronze and Iron Age Canaan.[21] Likewise, Laurel Koepf-Taylor's work survey's the studies of several scholars. Similarly to Steinberg, Koepf-Taylor also concludes the parameters of childhood are derived from the social context. She further concludes, "[. . .] it has become clear that at this time scholars cannot objectively study children; we can only study childhoods, the varying social constructions within which children function and adults relate to children and their own childhood memories."[22]

CHILDREN IN THE BIBLICAL WORLD

Naomi Steinberg convincingly supports the conception of childhood as deeply espoused in a cultural context. Therefore, a universal definition or perception is non-existent.[23] This is echoed in the earlier research of Chris Jenks who states, "Childhood [. . .] always relates to a particular cultural setting."[24] Furthermore, Steinberg goes on to support that the contemporary westernized perception of childhood as a protected period of emotional and physical innocence is not globally accepted.[25] It is further noted that a modern conception of childhood anachronistically applied to children described in biblical literature is impractical and

19. Harris, et al., *TWOT*, 254.
20. Ibid., 3289a.
21. Garroway, *Children*.
22. Keopf-Taylor, *Give Me Children*, 10–11.
23. Steinberg, *World of the Child*, xi.
24. Jenks, *Childhood*, 3.
25. Steinberg, *World of the Child*, xviii.

incongruous. Like Steinberg, Laurel Keopf-Taylor stipulates the conception of childhood is socially constructed.[26]

Economic Value

Recognizing the social construction of childhood and the differences associated to one's perception of childhood are critical when exegeting the biblical text pertaining to the religious education of children. Studies, such as David Patersen's, "Genesis and Family Values,"[27] presently exist that discuss the variations in marital patterns such as monogamy,[28] serial monogamy,[29] polygamy,[30] and polycoity.[31] Each of these patterns likely produce variations in child status within the corresponding household. "Understanding the fundamental role of the relationship between the socioeconomic status of mothers and the children they bore in the construction of the Terahite patrilineage is a central way to grasp the diversity of childhoods depicted in the Hebrew Bible."[32]

Likewise, children within the same home may be exposed to variations in childhood experiences. The biblical text illustrates that the firstborn son, within each household, receives a double portion of the inheritance as well as the right to carry on the father's name.[33] For some children, the social status of the mother bears more on the outcome of the child's status than birth order as observed through Ishmael. Though Ishmael is the first-born son of Abram, the lower social status of Hagar, in comparison to Sarah, results in the favoritism of Isaac. Though Isaac is the second born son of Abraham, he is the firstborn son of Sarah.

26. Keopf-Taylor, *Give Me Children*, 2.

27. Petersen, "Genesis and Family Values."

28. Monogamy is a term defining the marriage of one male and one female. This is observed in Moses' marriage with Zipporah.

29. Serial monogamy refers to a marriage in which one spouse remarries after the death of the initial marriage partner. This is observed in Abraham's marriage to Keturah after Sarah's death.

30. Polygamy is a term defining the marriage of one male to multiple females of equal status. This is observed in David's marriages to Michal, Abigail, Bathsheba, and Haggith.

31. Polycoity is a term defining the marriage of one male to multiple females of unequal status. This is observed in Jacob's marriage to Leah and Rachel, who differ in status from Bilhah and Zilpah.

32. Steinberg, *World of the Child*, 54.

33. See Gen. 25:25–26 and Deut. 21:15–17.

Hagar's lower social status results in Abraham's preference of Sarah and her demands to ensure the entitlement of Isaac to the family's inheritance and lineage distinction. Later Israelite law forbid this type of inheritance discrimination to sons of different mothers.[34] Similarly, Isaac's twin sons experience different preference from their parents. Esau is favored by Isaac, while Rebekah favors Jacob.[35] As the story illustrates, Jacob's mother goes so far as to help him plot the cunning apprehension of the birthright blessing from the elder twin.[36] In review of the biblical texts describing sibling and parental relationships, a uniform construction of childhood experience is not available within the biblical text. Anomalies between parents and children from one family to the next create ambiguous parameters on which to determine explicit conceptions of the child's role and status within the family. Variations in social status of mothers, birth order discrimination, gender discrimination, and parental preference for children—including children born of different mothers as well as preference for children born of the same mother results in a wide range of the cultural constructions of childhood perceptions as well as experiences among children within the same social community. Steinberg suggests,

> The construction of childhood in ancient Israelite society presumed the family unit was more important than the child, yet the family could not survive without the child. A male child whose survival did nothing to carry forward the patrilineage had little value for the family—as the position of Ishmael in the family household of Abraham, after the birth of Isaac, makes patently clear. Thus, the meaning of childhood must have been defined by the place of children in furthering the economic functions of production and reproduction for the family."[37]

Therefore, since a universal construction is not available from the biblical text, it becomes incumbent to consider the learning environment and pedagogical features for training children within each text on its own terms within the specific context of each text.

While childhood experiences may vary extensively based on birth order, gender, and parental preference, scholars generally agree on the overall economic value attributed to male children within the Hebrew

---

34. Deut. 21:15–17.
35. Gen. 25:28.
36. Gen. 27:1–29.
37. Steinberg, *World of the Child*, 57.

Bible. As an agricultural society, the wealth of the family depended heavily of their ability to sow and harvest crops from the land. Therefore, more sons born within a family resulted in the added ability to increase wealth and status. Likewise, it was traditionally the sons who stayed with the family, thus continuing the family's ability to farm through multigenerational family units consisting of a "household." Furthermore, it was often the son who remained to protect and care for the parents as they aged. As a result, sons were preferred for their economic contribution and ability to maintain the acquisition of inheritable property.

Daughters, on the other hand, bear a reduced economic value. While they could assist the family with some chores they were limited in their abilities and range of skills in comparison to sons. Because of their diminished capacity, daughters are subject to the harsh reality of lower socio-economic status than their male counterparts. This is distinctly observable is many of the laws that allow for harsh punishments for minor infractions in comparison to much lesser consequences for the same violations made by men.[38] Even laws that seemingly protect females from assault are more accurately a reflection of protecting the man's property interest of the women in his possession.[39] Victor Matthews further points out that the various titles used for women in the Hebrew Bible such as: virgin, harlot, concubine, wife, and queen, do not necessarily denote her moral status but rather her economic status.[40]

One distinction between the children of the biblical world to that of present day westernized culture is the value placed on the child in terms of economic revenue. Within the biblical texts, the imagery used for community annihilation frequently centers on the extermination of children. Regardless of social context, the violent death of children bears the burden of loss. While it is accepted that early societies often endure high mortality of children, the purposeful brutal death of children reflected in the biblical text suggests an additional threat of community and cultural extinction.[41] Keopf-Taylor convincingly points out, "the parallelism between offspring and other valuable produce in the context of destruction points to the necessity of both for survival and the threat that

---

38. Frymer-Kensky, "Gender and Law," 20.
39. Deut. 22:23–29.
40. Matthews, "Honor and Shame," 98.
41. Keopf-Taylor, *Give Me Children*, 99.

destruction poses to the community when children are in danger."[42] Texts such as: 2 Kgs. 8:12; Ps. 137:9; Isa. 13:18; and Nah. 3:10 reflect a pattern of community destruction with the tragic and brutal loss of children within the community. In essence, the loss of a generation (children) results in the obliteration of a people.[43]

Social Identity

Similarly to the social contribution, education of the child benefited the community, rather than the individual.[44] The biblical text offers several examples of preoccupation with the religious instruction of children for the purpose of ensuring the continuation of the community's ethos. This is supported in text such as: Gen. 18:19; Exod. 12:26–27; 13:8; Deut. 4:10; 6:7; 11:18–19; Ps. 78:1–7; Prov. 22:6; Isa. 28:9–10. The Israelite community rightly focuses on the education of both adults and children in order to ensure the survival of their religious ideals (ethos) and culture. An ethos is a defined philosophical worldview by a group of people or community. Communication and expression between individuals expresses the ethos as does the content of communication, expertise, and integrity of individuals and/or group.

One key text where readers may observe the importance placed on religious education is located in Deut. 11:2–7. In the context of this pericope, the Israelite nation is encamped on the plains of Moab. The character Moses, seemingly recognizes the people must prepare themselves to enter into the Promised Land. Since Moses is forbidden to enter with them, his death is imminent. Therefore, he issues a series of speeches for the Israelites, in preparation for what lies ahead. Within these speeches, he emphasizes the existence of the nation depends heavily on the education of younger generations in the testimonies of the elders and generations past. He reminds them of the Sinai covenant and that ignorance or blatant disregard of the covenant results in severance from relationship with Yahweh. The retributive theology of curses for those who disobey and blessing for those who remain loyal to the covenantal obligations is underscored with the reminder to teach the youth to obey the religious obligations of the law. Here, the adults are instructed to recall and

---

42. Ibid., 100.
43. Ibid., 101.
44. Ibid., 67.

retell their experiences at Sinai with those who did not experience it firsthand. In addition to this testimony, Deuteronomy 6–11 promotes the systematic instruction of religious expectations from parents to children throughout routine activities, similarly to the exposure children receive for other cultural norms. If they fail in their ability to learn from these instructions, they ultimately stand to lose the greatness of their national identity.[45]

Deuteronomy strongly presents the importance for educating the younger generation. The fruition of the covenant, the promise of land, and fullness of the blessing is contingent on the nation's obedience to the religious laws. It is therefore incumbent for the elders to accept this responsibility of religious instructions for the youth. The memory of their lived experiences and knowledge must somehow be transferred to those who do not know.

RELIGIOUS EDUCATION AND THE SOCIAL CONTEXT

The use of formal education in Israelite culture during the time of the writing of Wisdom Literature is an ongoing discussion among scholars with arguments for and against the use of formal education systems. James Crenshaw remains one of the leading scholars in this field as he examines early Israelite literacy and its transformation into a robust literate culture.

Wisdom's attitude toward reality is the worldview that reaches beyond the Fertile Crescent. This worldview is the fundamental assumption that one God embedded truth in all reality. It is thus the human responsibility to search for this truth. Within this background, the coherence of common problems and the bold address of life's inequities takes shape. All action has implications; therefore, it is necessary to find the ultimate source for insight. The understanding of reality is evaluated against practical everyday living as well as developing religious implications of action and response. In a society where the action of one impacts the greater community, focused training on behavior, decorum, and religious ethos is central to the training and development of children. Important questions regarding what brings happiness in turn shapes the ongoing education from one generation to the next. Central to the education within Israel is the theological ethos of the fear of the Lord as the locust of moral conviction and legitimate basis

---

45. Ridderbos, *Deuteronomy*, 84.

for not only religious instructions, but basic education in the rules of conduct. Proverbs strongly reinforces expected social interactions with lessons learned through social values and religious expectations.

As James Crenshaw shows through his research, the formal educational system is not strongly integrated into the Israelite community until as early as the reign of Solomon but possibly as late as the reign of Hezekiah.[46] Prior to this, education is primarily available only to the male children of the wealthy elite. There is reasonable evidence that these early schools were modeled after the Sumer and Egyptian schools that focus primarily on writing.[47]

Similar characteristics of the early scribal schools are found within the Wisdom texts of the Hebrew Bible. Examples such as Proverbs and its inclusion of moral instructions for civic engagement include aspects of traditional wisdom of earlier scribes in the tenth and seventh centuries B.C.[48] Additionally, its shared literature with older Egyptian texts point to the role of scribes in disseminating information to wider audiences. These scribes were responsible for mastering multiple languages with the added complication of complex vocabularies and the different Egyptian writing types (hieroglyphic, hieratic, and demotic).[49] This intricacy made formal education difficult to attain with less than one percent of the total population completing the rigorous honor.[50] However, this elite class of individuals makes significant contributions to traditions that cross international boundaries and cultures.

The primary obligation of the scribe is a civil servant responsible for recording the legislative decrees of the king. They later became responsible for overseeing other legal mandates, accounting, archives, and the recording of theological creed. While the importance of the scribal community cannot be over emphasized, the scribal education focused on literacy. Its fundamental role was ensuring the ongoing accuracy of written records. Very few prominent children had the opportunity to receive formal literacy training, and even fewer achieved recognition as vocational scribes. All other education relating to religious training and more practical vocations, such as agriculture, remained the responsibility of the family unit.

---

46. Crenshaw, "Education," 609.
47. Bromiley, "Education."
48. Marrou, *A History of Education in Antiquity*, xiv.
49. Ibid., xv.
50. Crenshaw, *Education in Ancient Israel*, 40.

The family remains the key source for instruction in ancient Israel. It is within the family that children learn the stories relating to their cultural and religious heritage as well as the expectations for character and moral standards. Respect, obedience, and social decorum are routinely modeled and discussed. As one of the core behaviors that disrupts the family unit, sexual misbehavior is addressed repeatedly. Indications of this are represented throughout Wisdom Literature where the dangers of foreign women and the result of deviating from the marriage partner are discussed at large. Moreover, with some anomalies, the cultural bias against women is also represented in Wisdom Literature, reflecting the religious prejudice that woman is responsible for spoiling the relationship between humanity and Yahweh.[51]

While there is evidence to support the use of formal education in Israelite culture, it is not pervasive. There is little to no conclusive evidence that validates the existence of these schools. There are brief mentions of schools, such as 2 Kgs. 6:1, but no substantial evidence for widespread schools beyond the training of the scribal community. Katherine Dell is correct in her summary and conclusion. Arguments for a robust formal education system in Israel, based on archeological evidence, remain unconvincing.[52] While there is evidence supporting literacy of individuals, there is not substantial evidence supporting where their literacy is achieved.

Therefore, there is strong scholarly consensus for informal education within the home. This education focuses on religious ideas and experiences that are conveyed through modeled behavior and oral tradition. Principles are amended to reflect the pertinent cultural mythos and ethos. Traditions from other cultures are adapted to reflect Israelite values and religious priorities as they are passed down to the proceeding generation. Essential texts are memorized so that learners of the religious traditions become living libraries par excellence.[53]

While studies in formal education systems are ongoing, their focus remains on validating their existence. There remains little attention on how religious ideals were passed from one generation to the next. Thus, the goal of this study is to systematically review the biblical Wisdom texts for evidence of pedagogical features and their use in religious education.

---

51. Crenshaw, *Old Testament Wisdom*, 15.
52. Dell, *Proverbs*, 26–28.
53. Gerhardsson, *Memory and Manuscript*, 95.

APPLICATION OF ACTIVE LEARNING THEORY TO RELIGIOUS EDUCATION OF CHILDREN IN BIBLICAL LITERATURE

The role of construction of childhood in relationship to religious education as described in the Hebrew Bible is the ability to contextualize the relationship between the teacher and learner. It fosters a mutual understanding of the role of children and the recognition of the expectations placed on youth by an elder generation. This conception of childhood and education gives way to the motivation for learning as the childhood moves toward adulthood and acceptance within the society. "Children and childhood in the ancient world were primarily associated with communal survival."[54] Part of this community acceptance is based on the child's ability to meet the social obligations communicated by the elders. This includes the ability to recite and act upon the religious ethos supported by the community.

As explained in chapter 1, learning occurs through a variety of means, both passive and active. Passive learning occurs when the learner is the recipient of information without active engagement. The role is solely to receive. Active learning, on the other hand, occurs when the learner participates in the learning environment through multiple senses as well as observation combined with inquiry or instruction. It was further noted that that studies support children's ability to learn through both physical experience and participation through imagination of role play through story. In this case, the learner participates in authentic learning through active imagination. Social interactions, testimony, and storytelling are part of the constructed social paradigms that create informal educational settings that transmits knowledge from one individual to another. The role of the child in these communities is directly related to the motivation of the elder generation to ensure religious history and ethos are passed to the younger generation. These dialogs and shared experiences become one of the means by which education occurs and is described within the Hebrew Bible. Learning from observation of human behavior creates long-term memory that is indiscriminate from learning firsthand through personal physical experience.[55]

Learning theorists such as Neil Fleming, Howard Gardner, and Jeanne Omrade agree that learners acquire knowledge in a variety of

---

54. Keopf-Taylor, *Give Me Children*, 32.
55. Bandura, "Social Cognitive Theory," 25.

ways. Within the Hebrew Bible, observable patterns of active learning are supported through the included descriptions portraying how religious expectations were taught to both child and adult faith adherents. Examples such as the memorizing of text through song, active participation in religious festivals and symbolism, as well as the observation of social customs are each illustrations of embedded descriptions of pedagogy within the Hebrew Bible.

As the following chapters will support, knowing (יָדַע *yada'*) Yahweh[56] is repeatedly described in the context of experiencing him. The semantic range for יָדַע reflects knowing through seeing. It means to learn through the senses including figurative, literal, euphemistically and inferentially.[57] Knowing Yahweh means experiencing him. Therefore, within the narratives of the Hebrew Bible, the writers and editors ensure the experiences of others are recorded for later generations. For those who did not experience it first hand, monuments are built in order to mark the location of pivotal events within their religious heritage such as the stacking of stones after the crossing of the Jordan River. Festivals are integrated into their religious calendar that allow later generations to remember and symbolically remember significant events such as observed in the feast of booths. These become markers, for later inquiry and testimony. Likewise, Wisdom Literature uses the same pedagogical features. However, instead of using story to record significant events and memorials, it uses the tangibility of nature and social traditions as visible pedagogical tools to teach the fundamental religious ethos of Yahweh's character. Once again, the most basic of tenets is communicated, to know (יָדַע) God is to experience him. These accounts and testimonies allow the readers to experience the pathos, ethos, and mythos of the faith community.

When oral instructions are combined with the other senses (taste, smell, sight, or touch), the learning becomes active and the younger generation participates in the experience portrayed by the elder generations. Knowledge and memory is created through action and social interaction. These combinations of learning through senses and social interaction are part of the conceptual framework of Active Learning and further described through the subcategories of the VARK learning theory and social cognitive theory discussed in chapter 1.

56. Deut. 4:35.
57. Harris, et al., *TWOT*, 848.

Within the construction of childhood, there are seldom examples of isolated verbal instructions that are not directly connected to an illustration that creates the pattern for active learning. The writers and editors of Wisdom Literature ensure the pedagogy for religious instructions is included to maintain the means for teaching later generations how to experience Yahweh and the persistence of orthodox religious instruction.

Chapter 4

Pedagogy of Job

THE PRECEDING CHAPTERS DISCUSSED some of the previously established studies related the discussion and definition of active and social learning theories as well as the relatively new area of study within biblical studies, construction of childhood. This chapter begins to address the informal instructional methods observable within Wisdom Literature. The data presented in this chapter will support the ongoing use of visual and kinesthetic teaching methods as well as evidence for social learning in reference to religions education.

The identity, relationship, and religious ethos of a generation is deeply dependent on the elder generation communicating its expectations. In the absence of ongoing instruction, newer generations must acquire information through trial and error rather than gaining previously learned content from those who already attained this knowledge. The religious community of Israel persistently accepts its obligation to share its mythos and ethos through the testimony of lived experiences and communal knowledge to both children and alien adults. As the faith community observes new insight into the nature of their relationship with Yahweh and self-identifies weaknesses within the nation, they incorporate this awareness into their pedagogical references. They observe critical events that shape their worldview and religious perspective and record them in such a way that these same insights and experiences continue to impact future generations of their religious and cultural heritage. As a result, mythos (basic values of a people) and logos (divine word) thus come together through religious education. Here, the sacred is juxtaposed with the memory of the experience. Though rarely explicit, the educational process for religious training is meticulously included in Wisdom Literature and is intimately connected to theological perspective.

The following chapters will argue that the form of the Wisdom corpus purposefully includes descriptions of a particular means for teaching religious expectations to later adherents of their faith community. The collected literature of Wisdom texts depicts essential pedagogical features for teaching religious ideals within the context of a social community.

Wisdom Literature offers didactic examples of instruction through its accounts of social decorum and portrayal of past evets. Knowledge is gained from the memory of past experiences that are shared as illustrations of moral attributes sought. The means by which the characters help others remember their religious and cultural obligations becomes part of an amassed interpretation of God's interaction with and expectations for humanity. The writers and editors record their own depictions as well as assimilate literature from foreign nations in such a way that they reconstruct the writing to represent and glorify their God as well as assert their theological identity.

Scholars remain divided on whether or not Job is a historical figure or purely a literary character. The purpose of this study remains rooted in the interest of educational learning theory and biblical texts that highlight pedagogical features. Therefore, the discussion of the Job text is restricted to the content within the final form of the text itself. No attempt is made here to engage the critical discussions regarding the genre or historical accuracy of the text. Questions relating to the historicity, or lack thereof, do not impact the presence of the pedagogical features contained within the biblical text.

The book of Job offers few specific references to teaching. However, multiple examples of active learning are included. Job uses nature, religious tradition, and the illustrations paralleled in the Pentateuch as pedagogical tools to define the religious ethos of the community. The text incorporates references to visual and tangible pedagogical features that enhance audible instructions or explanations. Additionally, the book encompasses an overarching use of social cognitive learning whereby the characters learn through the success and failures of those around them.

Job uses a variety of literary types, such as judicial, lament and dialog, throughout the text. Like narrative prose, Job includes a plot, conflict, climax, and resolution. However, it is mainly composed of poetry to communicate its story. One of its most noted literary features is the narrative frames that surround the poetry. These frames form the introduction[1] and conclusion.[2] As poetry, its genre contains specific conventions such as imagery and parallelism that demand genre specific reading and interpretation. The limited use of words in poetry creates purposed ambiguity that requires the reader to slow down and take note of the word and sound plays incorporated into the text.

As a whole, the book of Job both reiterates and challenges the ideals of retribution. Within the text, Job's friends affirm their support of Israel's sapiential tradition and the reliability of Yahweh's providence over them. Their monologues toward Job demonstrate their reliance on tradition and religious perceptions ratified in the Pentateuch and Deuteronomistic History, namely that Yahweh judges the actions of people and responds accordingly with either blessings or curses. This reliance leads to their conclusion that Job's suffering is clearly a result of his disobedience to Yahweh's laws. William Brown is correct in his assessment, Job's character is portrayed as a "clash of wisdom models" in comparison to his three friends.[3] The incorporation of "traditional wisdom" from the perspective of retributive theology is most pronounced in Bildad's speeches. Bildad appeals to Job to "Inquire of past generations, and consider the things searched out by their fathers [. . .] Will they not teach you and tell you, and bring forth words from their minds?"[4] Here, Bildad urges Job to heed the instructions of elders from generations passed as the ethos of traditional wisdom.[5] Eliphaz likewise shows evidence of his reliance on retributive theology in 4:7 when he asks Job whether those who upheld Yahweh's laws have perished.

Job, on the other hand, challenges this pious mindset and confronts the logic of his friends. Throughout his monologues, Job insists that the actions afforded to him are unjust and his adversity is not a result of his moral failure. Walter Brueggemann asserts, "For his part, Job's *integrity* is such that he will not deny his own lived reality in order to preserve the tradition of 'orthodoxy' or to maintain the reputation of God."[6] Job poses

---

1. Job 1:1—3:1.
2. Job 42:7–17.
3. Brown, *Character*, 63.
4. Job 8:8, 10.
5. Brown, *Character*, 64.
6. Brueggemann, *Introduction*, 295.

an anomaly for his friends that requires them to assess the fundamental cultural framework of their traditional wisdom.[7]

Though both an affirmation and challenge to the theology of retribution is explored in the book of Job, it is inaccurate to conclude that this book rejects divine retribution. The general acceptance of retribution is upheld throughout the book, particularly in the restoration of blessing to Job in the final chapter. Daniel Estes correctly identifies that one of the principles taught in Job is that Yahweh's actions do not always align with humanity's predetermined categories. Theology becomes anthropology if the actions of Yahweh are defined by human behavior.[8] "The book does not end with a neat, tight answer, but instead leads back to faith in Yahweh. All questions, even those beyond human comprehension, find their ultimate answer in God himself."[9]

A resolution for the differing presuppositions between Job and his friends is not directly addressed in the text. Instead, the text offers a meditation on the reality of humanity's limitation to obtain wisdom and that the wisdom possessed by Yahweh far exceeds human potential. Though humans can become wise and gain the ability to discern matters of the world through their relationship with Yahweh, even this wisdom is arbitrary compared to the wisdom of Yahweh himself. The indication is that neither Job nor his friends are able to fully comprehend the account told in the book of Job.

The didactic nature of the book of Job includes literary techniques such as repetition and rhetorical questions to captivate the audience's attention and advance the theological premise of the book. However, in addition to this, Job includes the use of specific pedagogical aids to assist the audience in retaining the religious education contained as well as offer a demonstration of the means by which they too can remember the theological presuppositions recounted in this book. The writers of Job use nature, history, and the Pentateuch to further define the religious ethos of the community and record the pedagogy through which this can be repeated for later faith adherents.

---

7. Brown, *Character*, 67.
8. Estes, *Hear My Son*, 26.
9. Ibid.

USE OF THE CONCEPT OF NATURE IN JOB

The character, Eliphaz, asserts his confidence that God destroys through an analogy of nature. He references the animal kingdom in Job 4. Though the lion roars with fierceness, he perishes for lack of food and the cubs are scattered. As Alter points out, even the greatest of beasts can be destroyed just as seemingly powerful men can be ruined.[10] This analogy is further reiterated in 38:39 as Yahweh questions Job, "Can you hunt the prey for the lion, or satisfy the appetite of the young lions?" The rhetorical question in 38:39 is used to remind Job, and subsequently mankind, of his place in the universe. The success of the hunt is dependent of the provision of Yahweh and beyond the scope of what man can provide. Within this analogy, the intangible lesson of God's providence is described through a tangible portrait, using nature as a means for describing one of the character traits of Yahweh. While this lesson itself is not in a setting for active learning, its initiative uses a principle from active learning in that it takes something that can be physically observed in order to teach an intangible concept.

In his response to Eliphaz, Job asks to be taught his wrongs. The word used in this context is יָרָה (*yarah*), which alludes to audible instruction rather than learning by doing or participating. However, a brief description of the use of nature in pedagogy occurs in Job 12:7–8. Here, readers are informed that the beasts, birds, fish and earth are agents through which learners gain insight to characteristics of Yahweh and his creation. The context of these verses is Job's first response to his three friends. However, the pronoun "you" is in the singular form in these verses. There is some debate concerning whether these verses are Job's quotation of his friends' statements rather his personal address to them. In other parts of the text, Job consistently addresses his friends in the second personal plural while they address Job in the second person singular. Regardless of the origination of these two verses, the pedagogy of nature remains effective. These two verses are part of Job's challenge to Bildad to ask the animals and nature whether Yahweh had dealt unjustly. His use of the ear and tongue suggests that he is comparing the wisdom of human rationale to the indiscriminate logic of nature.[11]

The words translated "teach" in verses seven and eight also derive from יָרָה (*yarah*). The common use of this word is to throw with control.

10. Alter, *Biblical Poetry*, 109.
11. Sneed, "Job," 432.

However, it also includes instruction that is likely verbal in nature.[12] It is the same word used in 1 Sam. 12:23 and 1 Kngs. 8:36. The word "tell," in verse 7, is translated from נָגַד (*nāgad*). Within the Hebrew Bible, it is used to describe both humanity's and Yahweh's revealing.[13] The word translated as declare in verse 8 is from סָפַר (*sōpēr*). This word literally means to count. In its Piel stem, it means to recount and acquires the idea of telling as demonstrated in Job 12:8.[14]

Within the content of Job's speech in Job 12:7–8, his character asserts that the world operates differently than the way his friends have argued. The wicked remain uncondemned and the innocent go unrewarded. While Job agrees with the ideals of retributive theology, he asserts that it does not occur. In support of his hypothesis, Job calls for the witness of nature. It is regretted that the author of Job does not describe how Job's appeal to nature will teach and inform his friends. Any further discussion for these specific verses would be speculative.[15]

However, the author does provide examples of nature's instructions later in Job 36. The focus begins in verse 22, when Elihu asks, "Who teaches like God?" He then goes on to proclaim that all of humanity has observed his work. Here Yahweh's sovereignty is unmistakably linked to his effectiveness as a teacher. Prior to this statement, the context is Elihu's admonition for Job to recognize and praise the greatness of God. Those who obey God are contrasted against those who refuse to listen to his commands. For them, the outcome is to die without knowledge.[16] Dying without knowledge reflects one of the worst tragedies from the perspective of Wisdom Literature. Yet, as the exalted teacher, Yahweh seeks to instruct humanity of his sovereignty through nature itself. Elihu goes on to include an illustration drawn from rain and storms as an analogy for Yahweh's provision. This theme of God's power in weather extends from 36:26—37:13. The power and might of the weather are conduits of revelation of God's greatness. In the context of the Hebrew Bible, this illustration is especially poignant as a contrast to the claims worshippers of Baal, who claim that their god, Baal, controls the weather and storms. Here, however, Elihu praises Yahweh as more powerful that this rival god.

---

12. Harris et al., *TWOT*, 910.
13. Ibid., 910.
14. Ibid., 910.
15. Longman, *Job*, 201.
16. Job 36:12.

Pedagogy of Job

Furthermore, he uses this common understanding of tangible power and might to acclaim Yahweh's ability to teach. It therefore stands to reason that Yahweh himself uses a tangible means and active learning pedagogy to capture the attention of the learner that they may identify the sovereignty and power of God through his control of nature itself.

Additional examples of instruction through nature are observable in Job 38–41. Here, Yahweh responds to Job's accusations and allows nature itself to teach Job. Animals are listed and discussed to expose the differences between Job's rationale and the wisdom of Yahweh.[17] In reference to the use of nature in these chapters, Robert Alter points out that the elements listed move from cosmology, to meteorology, and end with zoology.[18] Throughout these chapters, the author antagonizes Job's character through the barrage of questions posed by Yahweh to emphatically illustrate the diminutiveness of Job (and vicariously all humanity) in comparison to the magnitude of the Creator, Yahweh. This is done through the comparisons of actions available to Yahweh in nature, such as producing the morning sun, which are unavailable to humanity. Through the speeches recorded in Job 38–40, Yahweh asserts his wisdom and power through the imagery of nature. Yahweh's control of nature is maintained and readers are reminded of their lack of understanding. The overall message of these three chapters is that wisdom is found only in Yahweh, who distributes it as He deems appropriate. The author uses elements available to readers as reminders of this teaching. The sun, sea, ox, and steed are all familiar tangible examples and reminders of this teaching. Similarly, the author has even carefully chosen familiar mythical animals from popular "Near Eastern mythology, which often speaks of sea monsters that threaten the creation order."[19]

Throughout chapters 38–41, Job is challenged to view himself in the proper perspective of his incompetence in comparison to the greatness of Yahweh. Prior to chapter 38, Job demanded an audience with God himself. In his series of questions, God prepares Job to reach the conclusion of his own ignorance and desperate wisdom, which can only come from God. In this test, God uses nature to help Job grasp the correlation between what is seen and unseen. In other words, the intangible character and providence of God is recognizable in creation itself. Though Job

---

17. Longman, *Job*, 425.
18. Alter, *Biblical Poetry*, 94.
19. Longman, *Job*, 454.

cannot see God, he can experience God through his providential control over nature. This encounter between God and Job initiates with God's question regarding Job's presence during creation itself. Without waiting for an answer, God proceeds to question Job on whether or not he is able to control the sea. Here, God is described as both nurturing the birth of the sea while also containing its chaos. Again, Job must note that he was not present with God during the creation of the world.[20] Likewise, Job is unable to dispel darkness with his own creation of light itself. This, once more, is only completed through the work of the Creator. The barrage of questions continue as God directs Job's attention to the skies and inquires whether Job stores the snow and hail, brings forth the rain, or lifts the constellations over the earth. The tone of this interrogation is not necessarily threatening but rather an effort to educate and bring Job to his own recognition of his impertinence.[21] As the educator in this pericope, Yahweh must find a means to help Job recognize the supremacy of God while at the same time accept his own limitations. To achieve this, he initiates a form of active learning. Through his rhetorical questions, Yahweh uses the tangibility of nature and concepts that Job has experienced in order to transfer his understanding of the greatness of creation itself and further magnify the one who controls it. This tangibility of nature is used to teach Job about the intangible nature of Yahweh.

Next, Yahweh moves from creation itself to the provision of food for its inhabitants. Though humanity may domesticate some animals, man cannot conceivably provide the food for all beasts, both wild and domestic. This is a responsibility only God can fulfill. Additionally, 39:13–30 describes God as the one who gives animals their traits and the instincts they need to survive. Even the animals that seem deficient in intelligence, such as the ostrich, are protected by God through his provision of instinct.

As Job remains silent, the monologue focuses on creatures of strength and might such as the leviathan and behemoth. The formidable characteristics of these creatures emphasize their power and Job's inability to control them. These monstrous beasts stand at the apex of strength. Within Job's world are unfathomable and untamable mysteries yet both of these enigmatic creatures are under Yahweh's control.

The common factor to the creatures described in chapters 38–41 is that Job (and thus humanity) is incompetent to create or control them.

---

20. Job 38:9–10.
21. Atkinson, *Job*, 145.

The fact that they exist bears witness to something outside of human power. The inescapable truth laid out to Job through the series of questions and descriptions is that the divine wisdom of God is beyond man's understanding and it is God's prerogative to bestow knowledge as he determines. While it is not specifically addressed within this pericope, the underlying subject of pedagogy exists through Yahweh's confrontation of Job. As mentioned above, in addition to rhetorical questions, Yahweh engages active learning in order to correct Job's religious ethos. The supremacy of God is intangible in and of itself. Therefore, Yahweh associates it with things Job can see and experience in order for him to transfer his understanding of supremacy of nature and creation to the greater supremacy of the one who creates and sustains it. Here, the embedded pedagogical feature is the use of active learning in religious education. Though the focus is clearly on Job's lack of understanding, the didactic role of the biblical text widens the audience to those who later hear and read the account. Thus, the pedagogical use of nature continues to influence other learners as they too reflect on the questions and descriptions included in the text.

USE OF RELIGIOUS TRADITION IN JOB

The use of religious tradition is evident within the book of Job. The formulation of the characters Bildad, Eliphaz, and Zophar clearly relies on Israelite traditions and the theology of retribution throughout their recorded dialogues with Job. Leo Purdue accurately addresses the prominence of the dialogue throughout the book of Job. It is within the dialogues between these three characters and Job that the passionate debate over retribution surfaces. Job assaults one of the fundamental religious ideals of the Israelite culture as he seeks to disprove the theology of retribution. He accuses his friends of foolishly upholding a senseless ideology of a just God. Refusing to concede, the friends counter with Job's iniquity that must have led to his deserved status of misfortune.[22]

The content of Job represents a bold theological debate concerning the unexplainable suffering of those who were obedient to Yahweh's laws. The Israelite tradition offered no suggestion as to why those innocent of sin suffered inequity. According to Perdue, "By denying the justice and mercy of God, the poet of Job launched a direct assault on the continuing

---

22. Perdue, *Wisdom*, 95.

remnants of sociopolitical power in the form of kingship and priesthood, based on a traditional theology."[23]

It is the character Eliphaz who initiates the resolution of Job. He too rejects Job's attack on tradition and retribution as he endorses Yahweh's justice and the use of suffering to prompt sinners to repent. He concedes that the righteous may experience distress, but this too is from Yahweh as a means of greater discipline.[24] He draws on the Israelite creation account to warn Job of the fate of those who rebel against Yahweh.[25]

PARALLELS WITH THE PENTATEUCH IN JOB

The book of Job affirms the notion of Yahweh as Creator as described in Genesis 1 and 2. The character Job has seemingly forgotten his place is lower than Yahweh during his confrontation of Yahweh's justice. While Gen. 1:27–28 indicates a special relationship between humanity and Yahweh, Job's character has superseded this privilege.[26] The text then recounts the means by which Yahweh corrects Job's irrational thinking so that he humbles himself and demonstrates a reverence, or fear, of Yahweh.

In addition to presenting Yahweh as the Creator and focus on creation, the book of Job clearly integrates retributive theology into the dialogs of Job's friends. Bildad, in particular, incorporates this into his argument with Job. On occasion, Job's friends accuse him of breaking portions of the law described within the Pentateuch. This is observable in Job 22:4–9 where the laws of pledges for the security of a load are addressed by Eliphaz.[27]

However, as a whole, specific references to the Pentateuchal narratives are minimal within the book of Job. There are brief references to Adam[28] and Noah.[29] While there are no major references or pedagogical uses of events adapted from the Pentateuch, Gary Smith discusses the fundamental acts of salvation and election of Israel that is documented in the Pentateuch and Deuteronomistic History as fundamental to the

23. Ibid.
24. Ibid., 102.
25. Ibid., 114.
26. Longman, *Job*, 451.
27. Exod. 22:25–27.
28. Job 31:33.
29. Job 12:15.

theological motif of God's sovereign rule and justice that is taught in Job.[30] Smith goes on to discuss this justice and freedom of Yahweh's rule as well as the fools characterized in the Wisdom corpus who fail to see the "full beauty of God's ways because they limited God's rule to an inadequate conception of his justice and freedom."[31] While his methodology is overly simplistic, Smith's conclusion is correct. The book of Job exemplifies the overarching theological assumptions of the cultic traditions of Israel as they are illustrated in the Pentateuch and Yahweh is free to rule over individuals, nations, and nature through his own wisdom and providential ordering.[32] This religious assumption is well defined within the Pentateuch through the accounts of creation, selection of a younger brother over his elder, and Egyptians plagues. It is also defined in the Deuteronomistic History through the military victories and defeats established at Yahweh's discretion and the selection of David over his elder brothers.

Additionally, Job integrates the laws and admonitions of Deuteronomy as well as a focus on righteousness. The theological framework of Job uniquely expresses Yahweh's relationship with his covenant people through the perspective of the characters. Though the theological perspectives of the speakers are at times contradictory, their understanding of reality serves as the underpinnings for a broader perspective of salvation history developed from the Torah.[33] Through their conversations with Job, their theological stance on God's greatness, infinite wisdom, and dominion are clear. They also confirm God's punishment of the wicked and blessings for the righteous as found in admonitions of Deuteronomy 28. Job, like his friends, confirms God's greatness, infinite wisdom, and dominion. However, he differs in his stance on God's justice. He does not endorse retributive theology as evidenced by his emphatic insistence that his is not guilty of a sin equivalent to the curse or judgement he received.[34] Elihu, on the other hand, rejects Job's defense. He, like the others, confirms God's greatness, infinite wisdom, and dominion. Like Job's other friends, Elihu also affirms God's justice. Yet, he goes on to support his argument by stating that God's knowledge is infinite and he is intimately involved in humanity in the midst of pain for the purpose of

30. Smith, "Is There a Place," 17.
31. Ibid., 19–20.
32. Ibid., 16.
33. Ibid., 11–12.
34. Job 10:6–7; 12:4; 19:7; 23:12; 27:4–6.

redemption.[35] Likewise, Yahweh's monologue endorses Elihu's speech by illustrating how his knowledge extends far beyond Job's.

However, it is through the perspective of the narrator that the audience learns the theological context for the mystery of Job's circumstance. Job is shown to be correct in his denial of his curse as a consequence of sin. The retributive theology of his friends is inadequate yet so is Job's insistence on injustice. God's greatness, infinite wisdom, and dominion are upheld as well as his justice when seen through the lens of actions only God observes.

Here, within Job, God's creation of Genesis, salvation and providence of Exodus, and laws governing blessings and curses collide and the reader learns the theological ethos of these key texts are not categorically separable but rather intertwine with one another. While God does bless those who obey and punish the wicked, there is an infinite knowledge base by which God governs with all sovereignty. While this is revealed through creation, humanity remains limited by its vastness. God's sovereign justice and salvific history remains intact despite the limitations of humanity to fully understand it.

> In the midst of negative circumstances, justice exists, but it is mysteriously tempered with divine wisdom and freedom. This perspective is a unique contribution that wisdom theology makes to [Old Testament] theology, and it is an essential part of a [holistic] understanding of God's rule. It forces [the reader] to step out in faith, humbly fearing God, knowing that God has the freedom to use his power and wisdom in ways that go beyond human understanding.[36]

SOCIAL COGNITIVE LEARNING IN JOB

Specific references to instructional methodology are difficult to defend from Job. Yet, this text does exemplify that Yahweh is free to rule over individuals, nations, and nature through his own wisdom and providential ordering.[37] However, examples of active learning that correlate with Fleming's VARK learning theory are present. This can be identified in examples such as its references to nature in Job 12:7–8 and Job 38–41.

---

35. Job 33:13–28.
36. Smith, "Is There a Place," 17.
37. Ibid., 16.

In these examples, the author/editor(s) of Job suggest nature (visual and kinesthetic) is an agent for learning the characteristics of Yahweh. Observation (visual) of religious tradition, specifically observing blessing/curses from divine retribution, is utilized as a pedagogical feature. This text also includes parallels with the traditions from the Pentateuch, such as account of Creation (aural stories and visual observation) to reiterate religious ethos. Each of these examples correlates with the VARK learning theory introduced by Neil Fleming under the larger conceptual framework of active learning theory.

However, these uses of active learning are secondary to the role of social cognitive learning presented in Job. Recognizing this aspect of the text derives in part from the dating of Job. There is existing discussion regarding the dating of the literary material and the completion of its final form by editors and redactors of the Wisdom corpus. Mark Larrimore offers a solid dialogue of the composition of Job that begins to give evidence to the timing of its authorship. In his study, he asserts the combination of prose and poetry create interpretive challenges. Additionally, there are a number of lexical words that only appear in the book of Job. Nevertheless, the biblical text shows to be relatively fixed with few syntactical changes occurring between the Targum of Job (a Dead Sea Scroll discovery) and the Masoretic text.[38] I further agree with Larrimore when he states that an awareness of Job's composition changes how it is read and its effective history.[39] The dating for this text remains a focus of continued debates. Scholars, such as Robert Lowth, defend a date of composition as early as the patriarchal period. This is based on some of the internal references such as the length of Job's life (140 years) that is similar to the early patriarchs Abraham (175 years), Isaac (180 years), and Jacob (147 years). Other internal references to nomadic people groups such as the Sabeans and Chaldeans as well as locations referenced within the text are consistent with the patriarchal period.[40] However, the language and syntax used within the book most certainly suggest a much later date. Most scholars who support the later date place its composition during the Persian period between the fourth and sixth centuries. Further support for the later date is the book's incorporation of borrowed words from other

---

38. Larrimore, *The Book of "Job,"* 6.
39. Ibid., 9.
40. Constable, "Job," 1.

languages that were prevalent during the Persian period.[41] Katherine Dell offers a compelling argument for pre-exilic development and post-exilic redactions using studies from Crenshaw, Childs, as well as several earlier scholars.[42] Given the grammatical and lexical composition, I concur with those who place Job's composition later. The early dating for the composition of Job is no longer widely held by scholars.[43] While I recognize the internal references to the patriarchal period, it is more likely that the story is written later using anachronistic references within the text as a result of stories adapted from oral tradition.

Returning to an earlier statement, settling the case for whether or not Job is a historical or fabricated character is not vital to its theological position or diatribe of retributive theology. Given its internal references, it seems the author "set" the story within the patriarchal period. For those who argue for its historicity, I would offer this account may have held a long tradition in oral storytelling before it is finally recorded at a later date. This gives a plausible explanation for both its anachronistic references mixed with newer syntax. On the other hand, those who oppose its historicity but value its literary composition can relate to a later author who purposefully creates a character that is set within the patriarchal time frame. In either choice, we find a character that is purposefully recorded in an earlier period than the original audience reading it. This begs the question on why the author made this choice. What value does this add to the text and, more importantly, the theological position and purpose for the account?

I believe one response to these questions is the recognition of the book's example of social cognitive learning that is embodied through the actions of Job's character. Accepting the later composition of Job places the final editing in the post-exilic period for Israel. As a community, they are in a theological revival from their tailspin experienced as a result of exile. Prior to their release, they are forced to come to grips with how their destruction occurred in the midst of their active covenants with Yahweh. They are promised to live long in a land, protection, and a Davidic king. Yet, as they sit in exile in Babylon, these promises are seemingly broken. Are they serving the true God? If Yahweh is truly God, is he good? Is he just?

---

41. Kraus, *The Book of Job*, xvi.
42. Dell, *Proverbs*, 1–17.
43. Longman, *Job*, 24.

As they return from captivity, under Persian control, the remnants of these theological questions likely remain. Slowly, the feeble heartbeat of their cultural and religious heritage begins to renew. They begin to rebuild and relearn their cultural identity independent of the Babylonian influences that had pervaded them. What will become of them now? Will they be destroyed before they can rebuild their cities? Perhaps in recognition and response to these questions, the story of Job is finalized. God is not unjust. Perhaps this text serves as a gentle reminder that the wicked were destroyed while the faithful were protected and became the Israelite remnant sent to exile. The focus is not the exile, the focus is God's favor that allowed them to live. "Behold, he is in your power, only spare his life."[44] As the story of Job defends, sometimes even the righteous experience pain and suffering. Job then becomes the embodiment of social learning, allowing the readers to follow the account and recognize their relationship in his identity.

Drawing on John Dewey's philosophy of imagination in education, imagination can be a reconstruction of problematic experiences that adjusts the roles and outcomes to productive memory. It enables us to adjust fragmented or incoherent situations into productive and lucid memory. As Dewey explains:

> The things most emphasized in imagination as it reshapes experience are things which are absent in reality. In the degree in which life is placid and easy, imagination is sluggish and bovine. In the degree in which life is uneasy and troubled, fancy is stirred to frame pictures of a contrary state of things. By reading the characteristic features of any man's castles in the air you can make a shrewd guess as to his underlying desires which are frustrated.[45]

The role of the imaginative inquiry is to bring about the imagined possibilities.

Consider the role of the book of Job as an account whereby the readers imagine themselves in the role of Job. Feeling wronged from their exile experiences, they too question justice. As they identify with Job, their imagination (through social cognitive learning) allows them to role play and vicariously incite charges against Yahweh's justice. They too vent their frustrations and indict the theological claims of retribution.

---

44. Job 2:6b.
45. Dewey, *Reconstruction in Philosophy*, 60.

The social constructs within the story become their own and they too experience the agony of a questioned identity. The pain of their exile is portrayed in Job's misery and question, "Is this pain worth my existence?"

Though the very images in Job, not only does the main teacher (Yahweh) model active learning and anchor his instructions in concrete examples for the readers to learn but they experience the same transformation personified in Job.

Can God be honored in adversity? The outcome from the account of Job is a resounding yes. Yet, as we see from the epilogue framing, Job's transformation is not the final word. Job is rewarded but not merely for his "good deeds." He is honored for his refusal to blind himself to his reality and accept the accusations of his friends. Though he questions God's justice, he relies heavily on his theological presupposition of the reliability of God's good character. As a result, readers find God's criticism of the three friends who spoke untruthfully about him. In an ironic twist, it is the friends who are judged and rescued as a result of *Job's* prayer.[46]

In Job, the author's brilliant use of social cognitive learning provokes the post-exilic readers' imagination to identify with the main character and construct a reality that affirms the religious ethos of the patriarchal forefathers, girded in a firm recognition of Yahweh's greatness and unquestionable goodness. In the recognition of the importance of imagination in social learning, Jennifer Bleazby affirms, "Imagination involves the construction of effective ideas and achievable ends it is not disconnected from reality. Ideas that ignore the facts of the situation are unlikely to be effective at purposefully reconstructing the situation."[47] Therefore, the role of imagination is to create situations that derive from the experiences. The imagined possibilities must be directly related to and interact with the facts of the situation. The result is an imagined reality that is just as meaningful as reality because it does not divert attention away from knowledge or reality.[48] This is supported by Dewey's research,

> The imagination is not necessarily the imaginary; that is, the unreal. The proper function of imagination is vision of realities that cannot be exhibited under existing conditions of sense-perception. Imagination supplements and deepens observations;

---

46. Job 42:7–8.
47. Bleazby, "Imagination, Thinking and Education," 2.
48. Ibid., 2.

only when it turns into the fanciful does it become a substitute for observation and lose logical force.[49]

Therefore, I submit the fundamental premise of Job allows its original audience to momentarily escape from their fears of imminent, pending punishment in a weakened post-exilic community. As they fear what they cannot explain, a book is recorded that addresses this same fear. In a different context, they learn through Job's character that suffering is not necessarily a product of their lack of faith. As they cleave to their desire to indict Yahweh and demand answers, they learn through Job that they can never probe the depths of his sovereign knowledge. They must learn to accept that their reality is part of an amassed plan that far exceeds their ability to understand. In recognition of God's character, their suffering is momentary. They, like Job, must hold fast to their theological presupposition that God is worthy to be worshiped in the midst of pain. Thus, they learn, not by a direct address of their condition, but through the social cognitive learning that is made available to them through the book of Job. Their imagination allows them to experience Job's transformation and accept his consequences as their own. In the mirroring of the story to their reality, they can accept what is imagined through the story and experience firsthand both the repercussions of accusations and reward of truth.

SUMMARY

Many read Job as one of the deepest reflections on human suffering in the Hebrew Canon.[50] It shakes, to the very core, those who affirm God's blessing to the faithful with the most unassuming of sentences, "Have you considered my servant Job?"[51] While the book contains few direct references to instruction, it includes some of the most profound examples of instruction through both its characters and literary artistry.

Job's three friends uphold the religious tradition of retributive theology. However, unwaivering in what he knows is true, Job finds himself unable to support this ethos and challenges not only its accuracy but challenges its foundation as he contests Yahweh's justice. This attention to religious tradition is used to drive the dialog cycles between Job and his friends.

49. Dewey, *How We Think*, 224.
50. Larrimore, *The Book of "Job,"* 4.
51. Job 1:8.

Additionally, the book of Job includes multiple examples of concrete illustrations that assist both the book's characters and readers in connecting intangible aspects of God's character and providential control with tangible examples of these features in action. These examples of active learning build in the larger context of the entire book that is used as a paradigm for social cognitive learning.

Within Job 36:22, readers are directly pointed to the main instructor within the text, Yahweh. It is here that Elihu asks, "Who teaches like God?" From this introduction, Yahweh proceeds to take central stage within the dialogues that follows. In these instructions, he uses the concrete example of nature as support for his sovereign control. Job and likewise humanity are unmistakenly instructed that Yahweh's control of experiences on earth is represented in his control of nature for it is only through God that the seas find their boundaries, the stars are numbered, and the wildest of beasts catch their prey. Yahweh's response to Job's accusations in Job 38–41 draws illustrations from nature to teach Job. These illustrations form a strong argument against Job. Likewise, readers learn that the pedagogy adopted by Yahweh himself is active learning through visible concrete examples. Job learns that though he cannot see God, he can see the effect of God through his sovereign control of nature. Thus, Job is able to transfer his knowledge from his experiences from the tangibility of nature and its greatness to better identify with the magnitude of the greatness of the one who created and controls it. The intangible character of Yahweh is learned through the tangible observations and experiences derived from nature.

Repeatedly in the book of Job, examples of active learning that correspond with Neil Flemming's VARK learning theory are represented. The conceptual framework for active learning is embedded through the unmistakable examples of concrete illustrations used to teach principles of religious ethos. These are directly identifiable in texts such as Job 12:7–8 and chapters 38–41 where observations (visual) and experiences (kinesthetic) are combined with monologues of religious instructions.

Finally, the entire literary structure of Job allows for an incredible use of social cognitive learning through Job's character. Through the description of events within this text, readers are enabled to learn from their actions and the positive or negative results that follow. However, the story itself seemingly stands contrary to retributive theology. Unlike Job, the readers are clearly informed of his blamelessness. Yet Job is steadfast in his personal defense and accusations against justice. Likewise, he is also steadfast in his resolute belief in Yahweh's goodness. Through the account, he learns to let go of his claims for injustice and affirm his recognition of ignorance in comparison to Yahweh's infinite knowledge. In the same way, the Israelite community can identify with the actions of Job. They, too, experience the frustration of unexplainable circumstances that leave them pleading for understanding. Through the transformation of Job, they conceivably learn the value of letting go of their claims of fear and distrust. In the mirroring of themselves within the story, they learn alongside of Job. What cannot be taught in oral instruction alone in revealed in active learning. The unseen becomes visible through story and imagination.

Chapter 5

Pedagogy of Proverbs

SIMILAR TO JOB, PROVERBS utilizes nature, religious tradition and parallels with the Pentateuch as pedagogical tools to reinforce religious ethos. As demonstrated in other biblical texts, the writers/editors of Proverbs include examples of active learning through visual and kinesthetic objects/events to enforce their theological perspective. As will be demonstrated, these examples will correspond to Flemings' VARK learning theory as well as soundly constructed examples of social cognitive theory.

Proverbs occupies a unique niche within the Hebrew Bible as it allows the readers to consider lessons learned by others within the social community. The recording of the proverb ensures the potent social factors are preserved for guidance in ambiguous situations.[1] The proliferate literary use of proverbs extends to extrabiblical literature and prevalently endorse culturally specific language and social values.[2] Richard Honeck further addresses the role of proverbs as he writes, "Proverbs also teach their hearers, children especially, a great deal about [language]."[3] He goes on to state,

> [. . .] proverbs provide implicit instruction in levels of meaning and cognitive flexibility. Language is ideally suited for these purposes. It can turn reality on it is head in a way that perception cannot. Perceptual illusions occur, but perceptual veridicality is the rule not the exception. When we perceive what seems

1. Honeck, *A Proverb in Mind*, 120.
2. Ibid., viii.
3. Ibid., 120.

like a tree, it usually does not turn out to be a dog. In contrast, language allows people to say one thing and mean another. Proverbs optimize this bifurcation. Yet, proverb comprehension also requires that what was said to be taken into account, using context and conversational rules of various kinds. Because proverbs are used in indirect ways and can diffuse responsibility for the pragmatic and social message, the listener is taught that language is a tool. Thus, proverbs may facilitate the development of crucial conversational skills. They may also teach metacomprehension skills that will allow the listener to detect and resolve discrepancies between their current understanding and a more appropriate understanding.[4]

It is thus widely recognized that proverbs provide a constructive role that juxtaposes religious ethos and social context. Through this text, readers are exposed to social expectations as well and the cultural values that are directly espoused from the religious laws and experiences that formulated the worldview of the writers.

USE OF THE CONCEPT OF NATURE IN PROVERBS

Proverbs is replete with the use of experiential learning as a means of pedagogy. The social setting for the book of Proverbs continues to be discussed in recent studies. Longman briefly explores the support for Von Rad's suggestion of the service of the Court. Textual association with Solomon and the "men of Hezekiah" assumes relationship with the court. Longman also acknowledges the origin of the wisdom of Proverbs with the existence of scribal schools. He goes on to briefly account for some of the support offered by A. Lemaire toward the archaeological evidence in favor of schools. Smaller social groups, such as farmers, are also explored as possible settings for the establishment of proverbial statements.[5] While the conversation regarding the social setting of the book of Proverbs continues, Crenshaw's assessment is correct when he states, "All [biblical] proverbs, whether similitudes or paradigms, were grounded in experience."[6] He goes on to define a proverb as "a short sentence founded on long experience, containing truth."[7] One of the strengths of Proverbs

4. Ibid.
5. Longman, *Proverbs*, 27.
6. Crenshaw, *Wisdom*, 56.
7. Ibid.

is that their insight is not dependent on the isolated experience of a single writer, but the collected traditions of a community of people. The didactic quality of this text itself reverberates with the expectation of obtaining logic from the experiences of one's community. Past generations are linked to younger members of the community through the instruction of the community's ethos. Traditional values, including religious expectations, are clearly defined and communicated.

A second strength of proverbs is the ability to verify their accuracy. Crenshaw is correct in his assessment that, fundamentally, proverbs rely on their "typicality for immediate cogency."[8] A strength of proverbs is the ability to test the truth conveyed through daily experiences, with unchanging results, to confirm their validity. "It follows that proverbs comprise the best single source for discovering cherished values in ancient Israel" and offer insight into their understanding of good and evil.[9] Brueggemann also attests to the theological properties of proverbs as "it refers every aspect of life to the rule of God."[10]

According to Von Rad, the most characteristic feature of Wisdom theology is the relationship between creation and humanity.[11] The writers incorporated physical signs to demonstrate their religious perception. Practical wisdom is established from the accumulation of experiences and formed into an articulation of their faith in Yahweh. These experiences are interpreted through their religious ethos and then incorporated into a pedagogy in which others are able to learn their ideals. Richard Honeck echoes this as he asserts the quintessential function of proverbs is to foster the learning of society values, expectations, roles, and norms.[12]

One means for incorporating nature into their pedagogy is the use of analogies and comparisons between living and non-living things. Prov. 25:14 illustrates this through its comparison of the deceptive bragging of an impending gift to the deception of threatening storm clouds that yield no rain. This proverb serves as a warning against the pretentious bragging while awaiting gifts or favors. Likewise, Prov. 26:2 draws an analogy from birds to articulate the ethos related to curses. According to the literature of Proverbs, curses are the expected outcome of neglecting Yahweh's laws.

---

8. Ibid., 57.
9. Ibid.
10. Brueggemann, *Introduction*, 307.
11. Von Rad, *Wisdom*, 301.
12. Honeck, *A Proverb in Mind*, 120.

This perception ultimately led to the perception of retribution, described above. Here, within this proverb, these religious ideals are reiterated, as a "curse without cause" is incomprehensible. It offers the reassurance that such a curse retains no effect.

Proverbs also draws from observations of insects and animals to draw conclusions of how humanity is to conduct itself, in accordance with religious laws. This may be observed in Prov. 30:24–28, where ants, rock badgers, locusts, and lizards are used as illustrations for desirous traits. Here, the four creatures selected are considered weak or small. Yet, the purpose of their record here is to compare wisdom with strength. Each of these four creatures is highlighted for the wisdom it uses. For example, the ant stores food while there is ample supply, in the summer, so that it can be later consumed in the winter, when food is scarce. The wise youth are instructed to act similarly in Prov. 10:5. Here, social expectations are taught through an observable, concrete form (the ant).

For the writer, the experiences of creation were considered divine experiences.[13] As Murphy states, "The theological implication is that the world is never experienced as purely secular, as apart from the Lord who controls it and who is revealed in it."[14] The essence of the Creation account is portrayed in Prov. 8:22–31. Here, "wisdom" is the agent through which Yahweh created. A narration of Wisdom's accomplishments, these verses begin with an emphasis on the creation of Wisdom prior to the creation of the world followed by the depiction of Wisdom's presence during the creation of the world.[15]

The mystery of this interrelationship between Wisdom and creation begins in verse 22, where wisdom is described as birthed or created by Yahweh. The focus of both verses 22 and 23 is the preeminence of Wisdom to the rest of Creation. Verses 24–25 next describe the concept of the state of pre-creation. It is here that the character, Wisdom, clearly indicates her presence prior to the first formation of material mass.[16] This is reiterated once more in verse 26.

The second portion of this pericope describes Wisdom's presence during the creation of the world during five specific acts: the establishment of the heavens, the setting of the seas' depths, the strengthening

---

13. Von Rad, *Wisdom*, 62.
14. Murphy, *Tree of Life*, 114.
15. Longman, *Proverbs*, 203.
16. Ibid., 206.

of the skies, positioning of springs, and the boundaries for the seas. Wisdom is further described as the "master workman" in verse 30. It is here implied that Wisdom was not only present but an active part of the creation process. Longman goes so far as to allow for Wisdom to be the "guiding force" in creation, according to the syntax of this verse. Wisdom is next described as the mediator between humanity and Yahweh in verse 31.[17]

Verses 32–36 move toward retributive theology with Wisdom's insistence that listening, watching, and ultimately obedience to her commands will result in blessings and positive outcomes while death and negative consequences await those who ignores Wisdom. As observed before, the ethos of blessings and curses, similar to Deuteronomy 28, are asserted here. Deut. 28:1 initiates the blessings as a reward for those who hear and obey the commands of Yahweh. The word used in this text for obey is שָׁמַע (shama`) which asserts that the audience is to hear or listen to the commands of Yahweh.[18] Second, they are told to "do" his commandments. "Do" is translated from עָשָׂה ('asah), which means to work or to bring about an effect.[19] Blessings are stated as an outcome for those who listen and do as Yahweh commands. On the other hand, Deut. 28:15 stipulates that curses will come to those who do not obey the commands of Yahweh. Likewise, Prov. 8:32–33 uses similar phrases as it encourages the reader. However, the emphasis is clearly on listening, שָׁמַע, as it is repeated three times in verses 32–34. While these verses include the expectation of "doing" the commands, the writer uses שָׁמַר (shamar), translated as "listen." The semantic range allows for this word to mean "observe." However, given the literary context, "retain" or "remember" is likely a better translation for its use in this passage.[20] Also, like Deut. 28:15, Prov. 8:36 specifies that those who do not obey will receive misfortune. Whereas Deuteronomy ascribes this to a lack of obedience, Proverbs clearly references this as "sin" by using הָטָא (chata').[21]

The voice of Wisdom, in Prov. 8:22–31, to men does not insinuate that women were excluded from the instruction. Rather, this further reinforces the feminine personification of Wisdom. The reference to her

---

17. Ibid., 207.
18. Harris, et al., *TWOT*, 2412.
19. Ibid., 1708–09.
20. Ibid., 2414.
21. Ibid., 638.

as a workman, in verse 30, implies her intimate relationship with Yahweh. Tremper Longman, III offers an interesting discussion of excerpts from Sirach and the New Testament to assert that the character, Wisdom, in Proverbs is the personification of Yahweh's wisdom and thus informs readers that He created through his wisdom.[22]

The use of this description in Proverbs 8 is a means for allowing the readers to "rediscover" their God as Creator through the observation of his work in creation itself. In humanity's quest for wisdom and relevance, Yahweh himself is personified as Wisdom and thus the very source of that which they seek to acquire. Yahweh is thus able to transcend to the tangibility of the created world. According to Von Rad, "It is a 'near' governed by the God who permeates the concrete world with which wisdom teachers are endlessly occupied, thus keeping together 'the experience of YHWH's alternative' and an 'experience of the world.'"[23] Experiencing creation is a means of experiencing God.

USE OF RELIGIOUS TRADITION IN PROVERBS

Before analyzing the use of religious tradition as a pedagogical tool in Proverbs, a few observations of the literary setting should be noted. Through its literary setting, the writer of Proverbs 1 specifically brings attention to the instructional atmosphere established between the characters and further emphasizes the included pedagogy. Following the introduction of the book, a parental figure initiates a series of instructions to a silent son.[24] The use of the word translated to English as "instruction" derives from מוּסָר (*mûsār*). It denotes a disciplinary nuance or rebuke.[25] Its use in Proverbs coincides with parental warnings, admonitions, and commands. The father's instructions highlight the hierarchical status between the parental figure and his son in contrast to the foolish peers of the son who depict themselves as social equals to their elders.[26] The father's instruction strategy is encouragement for his son to observe the actions of his son's peers and witness the consequences for their poor

---

22. Longman, *Proverbs*, 209–212.
23. Von Rad, *Wisdom*, 62.
24. Prov. 1:8.
25. Harris, et al., *TWOT*, 877b.
26. Brown, *Character*, 30.

choices.²⁷ The father promotes the peers' actions as a greedy scheme that ultimately ends in self-destruction.²⁸

In addition to instruction from the parental figure, Proverbs also records instructions from the character, Wisdom. Wisdom's opening discourse follows the parent's discourse in Proverbs 1. Whereas the father addresses his own son, Wisdom addresses the "naïve ones."²⁹ This speech extends the father's discourse within the literary unit from the son to the community.³⁰ Brown explains, "Rather than mitigating the father's authoritative stance, wisdom heightens the hierarchical relationship between teacher and student."³¹ Wisdom's more critical stance against the scoffers referred to by the father reinforces the hierarchical relationship between the wise and the immature.³² The literary context supports that the son overhears Wisdom's discourse and her indictment against his peers that is shared with his father. The son is thus prepared for the character profiles that follow within the remaining literary units.

The pedagogy recorded in Proverbs is observation of others' actions followed by verbal instruction.³³ The son, or learner, is challenged to observe the physical world of human behavior in society in order to gain immediate insight of the outcome of one's actions. According to Estes, "Beginning with the premise that the world is created by Yahweh demonstrates order, the pedagogy of wisdom observes the physical world and then draws inferences for human behavior from what it sees."³⁴ The use of tradition, in conjunction with the observation of social activity, allows the learner to draw upon a larger unit of knowledge. Estes continues, "Through attention to what others have observed, the learner is able to

---

27. While the focus here is prevalently on the role of the father, it is acknowledged that the mother also likely participates in the religious instruction of her children. This also accounts for the mother's primary role during her children's early explorative years. However, because Proverbs does not directly address the mother's role in religious education, ongoing descriptions become speculative and debatable. Proverbs 31 does address the role of a good wife and the value she adds to the home. Here, she is described as having wisdom. However, it does not go on to directly describe her in a teaching role.

28. Prov. 1:19.
29. Prov. 1:22.
30. Brown, *Character*, 32.
31. Ibid.
32. Ibid.
33. Ibid., 31.
34. Estes, *Hear My Son*, 88.

augment what he himself has discovered through experience."[35] In other words, the learner is expected to accumulate knowledge from not only his own observations, but the collective observations of his ancestors and community. An example of this is located in Prov. 7:6–23, where the learner is expected to heed the counsel of his teacher based on his teacher's own observation of a demoralizing outcome with an adulteress.

On a different occasion, the teacher communicates the knowledge of observations he received from his own teacher, which is now transmitted to his learner.[36] The learner is expected to acquire knowledge from his own experiences and observations as well as the testimony or tradition of others. Throughout Proverbs, the teacher repeatedly encourages the learner to learn from tradition as a reliable source of knowledge.[37]

Leo Perdue also argues for the use of tradition in the pedagogy of Proverbs. He writes:

> For the sages, the knowledge of God came through the tradition of the ancestors; observation of the cosmos, society, and human experience; reflection on and remembrance of sapiential teachings and experience; rational analysis that was in part related to the understanding that there were connections between elements in nature; and the activation of the imagination of means of key metaphors. [. . .] All knowledge, including knowledge of God, is revealed through the order of creation, the tradition of the ancestors, and the sapiential imagination that begins with the perception of creation and the memories of tradition, but then moves into other areas: critical reflection, redescription of reality, and the rendering of God and human existence.[38]

Perdue's assessment of the pedagogy recorded in Proverbs is correct. The primary means for gaining insight is through observations using one's senses. The learner is able to visually see the outcome of another's action and determine whether these actions are acceptable to Yahweh based on the blessing or curse that followed. These observations and personal experiences are juxtaposed with the instructions offered by the teacher as well as the transmitted tradition of the community. The religious ethos and expected character morals are linked through this pattern of experience and verbal communication.

35. Ibid., 92.
36. Prov. 4:3–4.
37. Estes, *Hear My Son*, 95.
38. Perdue, *Wisdom*, 65.

Proverbs also records the actions of the father as a visual representation of Yahweh's actions. This is observable in 3:11–12. The father warns his son to heed the correction of Yahweh in the same manner that he would heed the correction of his father because, like a father, Yahweh corrects out of love. He does not want humanity to continue in self-destructive behavior. The literary imagery of Yahweh as a father figure assists with the comprehension of the purpose of Yahweh's correction. As Longman explains, "Correction, though painful, is thus seen as a favor, a sign of grace."[39]

The context of 3:11–12 is situated in the broader unit of five exhortations that mention the benefit of ideal behavior. This "correct" behavior is that which is conformed to Yahweh's laws. Katherine Dell argues that the final suggestion of fatherly discipline by Yahweh is a sixth component of this unit since it breaks thematically, not structurally, from the prior five four-line exhortations.[40] The opening admonition to remember the instructions of the teacher is reiterated throughout Proverbs.[41] However, this context heightens the instruction to specify the religious nature of these moral teachings. Here, ethical behavior is rationalized as the expected outcome of religious ideals.

Like Dell, Stuart Weeks also comments on the parallel use of the father as an imagery for Yahweh in Proverbs. He first discusses the father's use of his own family patriarchal heritage. Weeks then goes on to account for the character Wisdom, and her terminology during instruction that mimics the words used earlier by the father character. He then rightly concludes:

> Since the father is apparently the speaker throughout, these characters are speaking within his speech: he is essentially telling stories about them. Perhaps deliberately, though, the boundaries are blurred at points, as in those cases where the father recalls the words of his own father, or Wisdom addresses her 'sons'. The overall effect is to give a much greater integration between narrative and teaching than is found in most instructions: general advice is illustrated by stories, or lent colour by speeches and settings.[42]

---

39. Longman, *Proverbs*, 135.
40. Dell, *Proverbs*, 36.
41. Prov. 1:9; 6:21; 7:3.
42. Weeks. *Instruction and Imagery*, 42.

In addition to this visual representation of the father, Weeks also addresses the imagery of the foreign woman and the imagery of the path that are presented within Proverbs. Both are already well articulated by previously published material such as Roland Murphy[43] and Nancy Nam Hoon Tan.[44] There is presently no scholarly dialog that challenges the use of visual imagery and metaphor within Proverbs. Thus, the use of observation and tradition as a pedagogical tool for religious instruction is recorded and traceable within this text.

PARALLELS WITH THE PENTATEUCH IN PROVERBS

From the Pentateuch, Proverbs shares literary themes with Deuteronomy. The laws recorded in Deuteronomy illustrate a broader context of ethics that advocate an overall social decorum such as the good treatment of slaves and widows. Its emphasis on humanitarian decorum in conjunction with obedience to the law is similar to the instructions of the father in Proverbs 1–9. Likewise, similarities regarding honoring one's parents and the just treatment of foreigners are also advocated in both texts.

Discussions concerning which way the dependence lies between Proverbs and Deuteronomy remain unresolved. A. Robert finds Proverbs dependent on Deuteronomy. Like Robert, William McKane also relates Proverbs as a free adaption of Deuteronomy.[45] However, Moshe Weinfeld and, later, R.N. Whybray argue that the author of Deuteronomy used the already existent language of Proverbs.[46] While it is generally agreed that a connection between Deuteronomy and Proverbs exists, there is not a consensus on which direction the influence occurred. Unlike his predecessors discussed above, Michael Fox allows for the possibility that the language used in both Deuteronomy and Proverbs were well known maxims and that both texts are independent of each other.[47] Nonetheless, Fox's theory remains largely unsupported by contemporary scholarship. Katherine Dell conservatively suggests that there is not enough textual evidence to verify which way the textual dependence falls.[48] I concede that

---

43. Murphy, *Tree of Life*.
44. Tan, *Foreign Woman*.
45. McKane, *Proverbs*, 326.
46. Whybray, *Proverbs*, 60.
47. Fox, *Proverbs*.
48. Dell, *Proverbs*,168.

it is quite possible that versions of both texts were still in various editorial phases with one another and both texts could have shared adaptations of one another at different points. Since the textual dependence of these texts is not significant to this research, it will not be further addressed.

The opening instructional texts of Proverbs 1–9 share several ideas presented in Deuteronomy. The teacher's appeal to "hear" echoes the intensity of Moses' speeches in Deuteronomy. Here, in Proverbs, קָשַׁב (*qashab*) is used to refer to the teacher's authoritative commands rather than the commandments of Yahweh.[49] Desiring that this son would do more than merely listen to a "speech" from the father, the author inserts a more specific word, "command." This word is more closely associated with the law of Yahweh and leaves readers with the conjecture of whether תּוֹרָה (*torah*) may be in mind. The second verse continues this intensification by encouraging the son to bend his ear and extend his heart. The father encourages more than the act of listening by requiring the son to connect his whole person (heart) and emphasizes a more cognitive process of engagement.[50] Here, the idiom is in the causative ("incline the heart") and reinforces the notion that the son must do more than merely pay attention to his father but desire and choose something.[51] Finally, the father anticipates that his son should not only cognitively engage in the commands he hears but must act upon them, as referenced in 1:3. The instructions continue from the father and arrive at an interesting injunction in verses 6–8. The son is told that the mouth of the Lord gives knowledge, understanding, and wisdom. However, Fox points out that Yahweh is not quoted in instructional Wisdom Literature and thus verse 6 does not imply verbal revelation.[52] Katherine Dell offers a different approach by pointing out the words of God's mouth is delivered by the father figure.[53] She states it is thus plausible that the father is Yahweh's mouthpiece and therefore, vicariously an extension of him throughout the text.[54]

Fox's article on the pedagogy of Proverbs 2 is intriguing. In that, it is counterintuitive to the research documented within this study. As Fox explains, Proverbs 2 introduces the neophyte to the logic of the

---

49. Harris, et al., *TWOT*, 2084.
50. Longman, *Proverbs*, 119.
51. Fox, "Pedagogy," 237.
52. Ibid., 238.
53. C.f. 2:1.
54. Longman, *Proverbs*, 120–21.

educational process and encourages him to search for wisdom. The introductory verses of the chapter carry the central message while the latter lesson is rhetorical and is used to illustrate these verses.[55] He goes on to discuss the two phases of education presented within Proverbs 2. First, the learner engages in rote incorporation of the father's teaching that is complemented by the learner's personal logic and inquiry. Second, Yahweh grants wisdom after the learner has engaged in the first stage.[56] Fox concludes, "The search for wisdom proceeds not through esoteric inquiries or even through religious devotions, but rather through eager absorption and pursuit of wisdom such as the father is teaching."[57]

The differences between Fox's research on Proverbs 2 and the research contained within this book center on the focus and nature of instruction discussed. Fox's pedagogy is centered on the use of מֹסָר (mûsār),[58] often translated as discipline or instruction.[59] The difficulty of this focus is that Fox explicitly states that Proverbs 2 is a self-contained pericope.[60] However, mûsār is not used within this chapter. Instead, the words used are "words" אֵמֶר (ʾemer),[61] "commandments" קָשַׁב (qashab),[62] "understanding" תָּבוּן (tabuwn),[63] and "discernment" בִּינָה (biynah).[64] Given Fox's conclusion, biynah is a seemingly more appropriate focal point than mûsār. While I agree with Fox's connection of mûsār with the admonitions that derive from the father character and the connection of Elohim in verse 5; this word choice is not necessarily out of context. However, biynah corresponds much more accurately with the incorporation of logic and intelligence that Fox concludes as the pedagogical training that is described in this chapter.

Fox focuses a broader approach of instruction and the generalization of wisdom and pedagogy that is presented in Proverbs 2. This research, on the other hand, has focused on pedagogy within the religious context. Therefore, Fox's conclusion is arbitrary to the wider context of

55. Fox, "Pedagogy," 241.
56. Ibid., 242.
57. Ibid., 243.
58. Ibid.
59. Harris, et al., *TWOT*, 4148.
60. Fox, "Pedagogy," 234.
61. Harris, et al., *TWOT*, 118a.
62. Ibid., 1887b.
63. Ibid., 239c.
64. Ibid., 239b.

the Pentateuch and Deuteronomistic History. Similarly to the Deuteronomistic connection of the use of "hear," earlier in the chapter, Prov. 2:12 uses the word תַּהְפֻּכוֹת (*tahpukah*) "perversity." This word is used frequently in Proverbs and is only found, outside this text, in Deut. 32:20.[65] The affixing of laws or instructions to one's body is found in Deuteronomy[66] and Proverbs,[67] as well as similarities in the theology of retribution presented as the reward or consequence of obedience and disobedience to these instructions. The reference to sitting and lying down in connection to wisdom is found in Prov. 3:24 as well as Deut. 6:7. Whereas Deuteronomy uses this in the context of meditating on the commands of Yahweh, Proverbs uses this in connection with walking in wisdom leading to the ability to walk and lie down without fear. Nevertheless, as noted by Dell, the language between these two texts is strikingly similar.[68] Similarity is also found through the expected outcome of adultery presented in both texts. Prov. 4:11–13 echoes the legal texts that describe death and destruction as the result of infidelity. Lev. 20:10 and Deut. 22:22 relate the same consequence for both adulterer and adulteress.

More important to this research is the use of education and pedagogy and the similarities found between Deuteronomy and Proverbs. Prov. 7:1–3 parallels several important factors in Deuteronomy. The context of these verses is an exhortation to heed the instructions that follow. The use of the phrase "my speech" is exceedingly significant. Katherine Dell and Tremper Longman, III[69] both accurately address the use of this phrase, in Proverbs, as a means to demonstrate the parental teaching analogous to the doctrines expressed in Deuteronomy. [70] The authority of the father is supported by the Mosaic Covenant and thus his "instruction" becomes indistinguishable from Yahweh's. [71] The phrases "apple of your eye" and "binding" of teachings also reflect Deuteronomistic terminology.[72]

The integration of religion and education, observable in both Deuteronomy and Proverbs, leads to a presumption that the educational content

---

65. Ibid., 512f.
66. Deut. 6:8.
67. Prov. 3:1–4; 6:21–22; 7:1–3.
68. Dell, *Proverbs*, 171.
69. Longman, *Proverbs*, 186.
70. Dell, *Proverbs*, 173.
71. Longman, *Proverbs*, 186.
72. Compare Prov. 7:2 with Deut. 32:10 and Prov. 7:3 with Deut. 6:8; 11:18.

of Proverbs 1–9 had religious affinity from its inception and that religious ideals are incorporated into the formation of character described in these nine chapters. Katherine Dell offers a strong discussion on the incorporation of Deuteronomy and Proverbs. She relates the cultic influence and social context of the community with the educational use of Proverbs 1–9. Furthermore, she demonstrates additional links between Deuteronomy and Proverbs in the latter chapters 10–31, though readily admits the similarities are more sparse than those present in Proverbs 1–9.

The incorporation of Deuteronomy with Proverbs does not include shared examples of tangible Pedagogy, as used elsewhere. The difficulty of assessing the use of the Pentateuch in Proverbs is that it does not share the same use of this content as it is used in other biblical texts. Whereas other Wisdom texts incorporate events described in the Pentateuch as a means of memory recall and tangible reminders of Yahweh's providence, Proverbs does not. There is no mention of redemptive history, the patriarchs or the exodus event. These widely used examples are peculiarly absent from Proverbs. However, this does not distract from the educational intent and religious instruction of Proverbs.

The examples of Deuteronomistic parallels in Proverbs are centered on the authoritative influence of Yahweh's commands and the appeal of the father figure to his son to rely on these precepts and theological implications. This is illustrated in Proverbs' use of "fear of the Yahweh." This phrase is first found in the introduction of the text, in Prov. 1:7. The position of this verse in the preamble signifies the editor's intention of teaching the readers that there is no knowledge/wisdom without a relationship with Yahweh. This relationship is characterized by reverence or "fear."[73] This phrase is notably found throughout the Pentateuch[74] as well as 1 Sam. 12:14 and 2 Kgs. 17:28. The use of this phrase, in Prov. 1:7, is the acknowledgment of the theocentric nature of knowledge/wisdom and the dependence on one's relationship with Yahweh as a condition for obtaining it. The advice offered throughout Proverbs cites experience, observation, and human reason as viable means for gaining knowledge. However, as presented in 1:7, even this is conditional on one's respect and relationship with Yahweh.

---

73. Longman, *Proverbs*, 57.
74. See Gen. 22:12; Exod. 3:16, 19:16; Deut. 5:29, 10:12, and 28:58.

SOCIAL COGNITIVE LEARNING IN PROVERBS

The use of social cognitive learning is strongly represented in the book of Proverbs. Social cognitive learning occurs through observation of the behaviors of others and learning from these experiences. Lev Semyonovich Vygotsky asserts that social interaction and cultural norms are important components for human learning. He further describes learning as cooperative and cultural as knowledge is gained primarily through the worldview established through one's culture and social relationships.[75] The modeling of behaviors becomes a form of engaging in active learning when the learner has the ability to inquire of the significance of his or her observations or receive oral instructions regarding their significance. This dynamic engagement of learner and instructor moves the observational learning from passive to active through the verbal exchange combined with the initial observation. It is also asserted that learning is further motivated through observing the reward and/or punishment associated with an observed behavior.[76]

One of the earliest examples of social cognitive learning in Proverbs occurs in the latter part of chapter 1. Here, the destruction that comes to fools is described as a contrast to the reward for the wise. While neither the character of the fool or wise is defined, the actions of such individuals receive brief descriptions. A second description begins in 2:16. In this description an example of a fool is identified as a wayward woman. Again, both her actions and the destruction that results from these actions are described. It is further described that any man who keeps company with a woman of this kind will likewise find destruction. Again, this is contrasted with the man who, instead, keeps company with good men. In contrast to the foolish man who reaps destruction, the good man reaps land and blamelessness.[77] Later in 6:12–15, the learner is given examples of actions from a wicked man. In the same context, the calamity that results from these actions are also described.

The instructor then moves to personal testimony of observations in Prov. 7:6–23. In this description, he retells the scene of an adulteress woman who waits in darkness for a naïve man who is unaware of the consequences of her company. He goes on to describe the cunning words she uses to lure him to take action that is defiant of the accepted religious

---

75. Li and Lam, "Cooperative Learning," 2.

76. Gage ad Berliner, *Educational Psychology*, 340.

77. Prov. 2:21.

and social norms of the community. The outcome, he states, is the cost of his life.[78] The instructor then follows this testimony with additional instructions to stay away from women of this character because she leads to sheol and death. In this pedagogical illustration, the writer combines both observation as well as follow-up instruction to achieve active learning through the social context. Instead of learning from the experiences first hand, the learner is enabled to learn through the observation of others. In addition to making personal observation, he is also enabled to vicariously observe through the eye witness account and testimony of the instructor who likewise goes on to clarify the actions in each of these examples. A second testimony is located in 24:30–34. Here, the writer records his observations of a field owned by a man with little conviction to work. Again, he follows up with instructions regarding the observed behavior, thus moving the example from passive to active learning.

Finally, not only does Proverbs include pedagogical examples of active learning through visible illustrations that align with the VARK learning theory and examples of social cognitive learning, but the book as a collective whole acts as a model for pedagogical teaching. Much like Job, discussed in the previous chapter, the book of Proverbs is "set" by the author/editor(s) as a loosely knit "story" that includes a father and son who serve as examples of instructor and learner. Within this account, readers gain a firsthand example of how to provide a child with religious education. Within the account, the reader observes example after example of specific visual illustrations that are used in combination with oral instruction. Additionally, the father/instructor gives several examples of observable behaviors for the son to learn both the positive and negative consequences result from either obedience or disobedience to religious laws that govern human behavior.

The speeches and poems of chapters 1–9 vigorously assert that the one who seeks after wisdom and action governed by religious laws is safeguarded from misstep and destruction. Ultimately, wisdom is a transcendent quality that comes from God.[79] Personified as a woman in chapters 8–9, wisdom seeks intimate companionship with those who desire her. However, the fools are those who are not persuaded and reject her companionship. They dismiss discipline through their arrogance and naivety. They therefore find destruction because they are not rewarded with

---

78. Prov. 7:23.
79. Prov. 2:6; 8:22–31.

wisdom's protection. The focus, then, is the learned behavior through contemplating traditional teaching with wisdom.[80] The specific situations are not its focus, but rather the connection of human choice rooted in religious ethos. It is the unfolding of human experience in light of God's redemptive plan and covenant promises. It is the role of obedience in the midst of free will.

SUMMARY

In conclusion, themes and interests of the Pentateuch are notably present in Proverbs. The extent to which they are used is also markedly different than their use in other texts. The educational intent of Proverbs is uncontested, as is the religious nature of the text. Pertinent to this research, it is already documented that Proverbs does use other tangible pedagogical tools, such as nature and first hand observation and experience. Unlike the remaining Wisdom corpus, Proverbs does not use the Pentateuch as a means of reminding readers of Yahweh's action in history or his supremacy. Instead, the Pentateuch is used as a means of equating the instructions of the father figure with those of Yahweh. It serves as a reminder of the instructions the readers have learned from instructions derived from Yahweh through the character, Moses and the Deuteronomistic literature.

The rationale for this comparison of authority remains theorized. It is repeated on more than one occasion throughout the text. According to Longman, "The authoritative nature of the father's speech is underlined by its being called 'commands' [...]. In other words, wisdom is thus identified with tradition passed down from father to son."[81] It is plausible this is used in connection to Yahweh's laws, but must remain speculative since there is not enough textual evidence to fully support it.

The book of Proverbs offers multiple examples of religious education that include pedagogical features. These instructional tools include the use of nature (visual) as described in Prov. 10:5, observation of human behavior and consequences (visual) as described in Prov. 7:6–23, and references to the law as described in Proverbs 1–9. These parallel with the Pentateuch include similar usage of "hear" that is comparable to its usage in Deuteronomy. Proverbs also includes descriptions of the

---

80. Hayes, *Proverbs*, 11.
81. Longman, *Proverbs*, 126.

effects of disobedience to the laws that parallel the Pentateuch such as the consequences of infidelity (visual and arguably kinesthetic) described in that correlate with the descriptions of Lev. 20:10 and Deut. 22:22. As demonstrated in other biblical texts, Proverbs incorporates active learning through to visual and kinesthetic pedagogical features that correlate with the VARK learning theory.

In addition to active learning, Proverbs includes strong examples of social cognitive learning where the learner is specially instructed to watch and learn from the behaviors of others. Examples include specific illustrations of actions and their results such as that observed in 6:12–15. Other examples of social learning include the use of personal testimony such as the example given from 7:6–23.

The character of an individual is a social construction and is inseparable from culture, it is significant that the literary text of Proverbs distinctly uses this phenomenon as a means for training character that is rooted from a religious ethos. Within this text, the reader identifies the concept of character as unmistakably connected to the religious expectations of the faith community. In a central contrast between wise and fool, just and unjust, righteous and wicked, Proverbs uses the communal constructions of social and religious expectations. It explores the implications of destructive behaviors such as adulty, mistreatment of others, bribery, and dishonesty as well as the product of conductive behaviors such as friendships, work ethic, child rearing, and marital relationships. Within this social construction, the intangible, abstract religious law becomes tangible through the learner's ability to observe the interrelation between action and consequence.

Chapter 6

Pedagogy of Ecclesiastes

THE PURPOSE FOR THE Ecclesiastes text lies at the very center of some of its interpretive challenges. Its internal tensions as well as inconsistencies with other texts within the Hebrew Bible require explicit attention to ensure consistent theology. Peter Enns is correct in his estimation when he states, "Indeed, perhaps no other book of the Hebrew Scriptures has had the history of counterunderstandings as Ecclesiates."[1] Fueled by these tensions, the reader must reach a conclusion. Has the character, Qoheleth, lost his faith or does he present a refreshing blunt realism? Is he the model character of wisdom learned through his observations and experiences or is he a wolf in sheep's clothing, the ultimate fool who has deceived even himself?[2]

Ecclesiastes describes the journey of humanity's quest to discern a meaningful pattern to daily experiences and desires. It emphasizes the importance of a theocentric worldview as the means for determining the ultimate purpose of humanity. Specifically, it targets youth and challenges them to choose a life surrendered to the commands of Yahweh. As with the wise and wayward women in Proverbs, Ecclesiastes presents choices that must be negotiated to achieve blessing and joy that is attributed to the instructions of Deut. 30:15–18.

> Practical wisdom, such as that found in most of Proverbs, endeavors to expound and illustrate the typical patterns observable in God's ordered world. In practical wisdom, the hearer is

1. Enns, *Ecclesiastes*, 3.
2. Ibid., 4.

challenged to find life by choosing wisdom and avoiding folly. The speculative wisdom of Ecclesiastes, as well as Job, supplements practical wisdom by addressing the enigmatic realities of life that cannot be subsumed under the typical retribution formula, which states that choosing wisdom leads to life and choosing folly leads to death.[3]

The purpose of Ecclesiastes is to demonstrate the necessity of a theocentric worldview for the explanation of all realities as well as propose the gravity of choosing an alternate idealism.[4] Unlike Proverbs, Ecclesiastes does not teach the specific responsibilities of faith. Instead, it more broadly teaches humanity's accountability to Yahweh and the social expectation of the promotion of others, rather than the self. The pedagogy expressed within this book highlights the continued use of tangible objects or activity as a means of education. The title itself renders the likeliness of is pedagogical inclusion. Ecclesiastes is the Latin translation of its Hebrew title, *Qoheleth*. This word properly means, "one who calls an assembly." This is often conveyed as "preacher" or "teacher." The suggestion presented is that of a wise sage to his pupils through the writings of the character Qoheleth. This teacher, characterized through Qoheleth, teaches more concretely than any of the other biblical texts.[5] He incorporates daily activities and experiences to tangibly express his ideals of humility. This broad topic or theme encompasses the subtopics of friendship, human authority, social justice, gerontology, and limitations of human wisdom.[6] All of this is discussed from the theological perspective (or ethos) of the writer, through the character, Qoheleth, which is to revere Yahweh. In addition to active learning, the writer incorporates social cognitive theory through his testimony of what he has personally observed in the actions of others and the consequences of these actions. He uses this pattern of action-consequence as a pedagogical feature for passing on his religious ideals.

The strategy of Qoheleth's character is to disband the illusions of his learners regarding their man centered worldview.[7] Through his own cynicism, he confronts the disappointments of "the real world." He exposes the useless pretensions of worldly achievements in order to offer

---

3. Estes, *Hear My Son*, 281.
4. Ibid.
5. Davis, *Proverbs, Ecclesiastes, and the Song of Songs*, 161.
6. Machinist, "Ecclesiastes," 1603.
7. Davis, *Proverbs, Ecclesiastes, and the Song of Songs*, 160.

a more grounded perspective of humility through the fear of Yahweh.[8] Human activity for the sake of activity lacks ultimate value. However, every experience, in light of Yahweh and fear of him, leads to unfathomable joy. Davis states, "Koheleth's insistence on taking pleasure expresses a genuinely religious form of humility, because it is God 'who makes everything' (11:5) and therefore ultimately it is God who enables every form of enjoyment."[9]

Ecclesiastes includes a variety of pedagogical features that includes visual and kinesthetic actions associated with Flemming's active learning theory. However, it dominantly uses social cognitive theory. The writer's persona of relating himself as a king allows him to explore through resources that are not available to the "common man." As a king, he is privileged to spend what others cannot earn and travel to estranged places where others dare not consider.[10] It is up to the reader to determine the wisdom of his testimony and learn from the behaviors of those he claims to have observed.

I agree with Peter Enns' discussion on the importance of the third person narrator of Ecclesiastes. Given the inner tension and cursory statements within the text, the interpreter must investigate the roll of this narrator, the framing of the text, and the textual interjections. He further asserts that a second author is plausible, the frame narrator, providing orthodox insertions to balance the unorthodox declarations of the first author with the overall ethos of the Hebrew Bible.[11] However, he goes on to explain, "We should take careful note that there is no indication here (or elsewhere in 1:1–11) of any attempt to correct or sanitize the tone of what will occupy the middle section of the book. The problems in interpretation arise at the very outset when we presume that of the frame narrator's words, even here, are a negative evaluation rather than simply a succinct summary of Qoheleth's words." Therefore, attention moves to the epilogue of the text in 12:8–14. Enns goes on to conclude the epilogue clearly establishes the frame narrator as the author himself. Here, the evaluative tone is not corrective of the theology but rather supports the observations described throughout the text. Therefore, the function of the frame narrator encourages a view that the narrator is the author.

8. Ibid., 161.
9. Ibid., 161–62.
10. Enns, *Ecclesiastes*, 15.
11. Ibid., 4.

As a result, Qoheleth is the character he uses as the vehicle for conveying his argument.[12] Ongoing discussions among scholars disclose a lack of consensus or the identity of Qoheleth. The arguments range from a historical character identified as King Solomon and author of Ecclesiastes to a fabricated character created by the author to build trust in readers. The identity of Qoheleth does not impact the theological implications of the text nor does it impact the use of pedagogical features within the text. Therefore, since this issue is not vital to this study, it is not further argued.

Internal references in Ecclesiastes claim Solomon's authorship. This claim remained largely undisputed until the eighteenth century. The rise in literary and historical criticism lead to widespread skepticism of the Solomonic authorship based on linguistic factors that are characteristic of the Persian period of the third and fourth centuries.[13] While the specific dating of the authorship is not fully resolved among scholars, there is a general consensus of this post-exilic composition.

Qoheleth reflects on the anxieties consistent with the emerging dilemmas in the post-exilic community. The arbitrary security and recognition of intangible uncertainties weigh heavily of the community of faith as they grapple with their role under the Persian system. Death, tragedy, and vicissitude are common fates for both the rich and poor, the wise and the fool. The writer uses the character, Qoheleth, to boldly address these realities with an unflinchingly realistic perspective.[14]

USE OF THE CONCEPT OF NATURE IN ECCLESIASTES

Ecclesiastes does not include strong use of nature as a pedagogical tool. However, as early as 1:3–7, the writer instructs the reader to consider the steadfast earth as a means for learning. Here, the reader is encouraged to consider the rising and setting of the sun, the blowing of the wind, and the cycling of water from the streams to the ocean and return to the sky. In each of these examples, the writer contends the earth continues to reset itself. It is steadfast and unchanging. Humanity, in contrast, labors and dies. However, like the water that falls, returns to the sky, and then falls again; so each generation replaces the one who preceded it. The argument is made in verses 8–11. There is nothing permanent, nor is there

---

12. Ibid., 6.
13. Constable, "Ecclesiastes," 1.
14. Brown, *Ecclesiastes*, 10.

new information conceived. This is learned by examining the consistent cycles observable in nature. Each cycle is incomplete in its own properties. Its ultimate purpose is derived from the Creator through its full course of action and the environment it impacts. Therefore, the ultimate meaning of life is not found in watching others; it is found only in the Creator.

In addition to the observations of the steadfast seasons, there are two additional texts that offer the strong examples of the use of nature as a pedagogical feature in Ecclesiastes. These include Eccl. 3:11–22 and 12:1–8. The repeated phrase, "a chasing after the wind," should also be considered for its consistent use to relate the attainment of wisdom throughout this text.

Within chapter 3, the writer of Ecclesiastes incorporates nature through his description of eternity within the hearts of humanity. He expresses confidence in Yahweh's timing of events and providential oversight of creation. Verse 14 articulates Yahweh's purpose of creation is for humanity to fear him. It is thereby presented that humanity is able to trust Yahweh and assure that nothing of substance perishes eternally because of the excellence of Yahweh's creation.[15] In other words, the perfection of what is observed in nature is evidence to what cannot be seen in eternity. Humanity learns to trust Yahweh through the reliability of the seasons[16] and learns to fear Yahweh through the flawlessness of his work.

The illustration of flies in perfume to convey the weight of foolishness is recorded in Eccl. 10:1. The writer's point is that one's personal wisdom is greatly diminished by the exhibit of foolishness, even at the most miniscule of appearances. This verse forms the conclusion of its preceded discussion in 9:13–18.

The use of nature is found again in Ecclesiastes 11 where the writer refers to various horticulture elements to emphasize the importance working diligently while relying on Yahweh's control of the conditions that bring fruitfulness to man's labor. From these illustrations drawn from nature, namely clouds, rain, and wind, the author illustrates the theme throughout the entire Ecclesiates text. Humanity cannot fathom Yahweh's plan and sovereign actions on humanity's behalf. However, the ethos defined by this author for his audience is that though man cannot comprehend and innately follow God's plan, he can follow God's

---

15. Davis, *Proverbs, Ecclesiastes, and the Song of Songs*, 185.
16. Eccl. 3:1–11.

PEDAGOGY OF ECCLESIASTES 103

instructions for daily living and thus bring about God's purpose through obedience to his laws. Since the future is unknown, the wise proceed to work with a comprehension that God's plan is unfolding and yields good fruit. Thus, here, the author instructs his audience through the visual and kinesthetic examples he draws from nature to disclose his ethos and religious expectations for conforming to the religious laws given to the Israelite community. The systematic routines of nature are unchanging, as is Yahweh's plan. Though circumstances in one's life unexpectedly change, the overall rhythm remains on track and religious obedience is expected.

This point is further emphasized though the literary echoes and repetitions throughout the book. The repeated attention to evil/painful tasks (עִנְיָן רַע, ra' 'inyen) in 1:13, 2:23, 4:8, and 5:14 is not made clear other than the overall emphasis on Yahweh's assignment of man's tasks as stated in Eccl. 3:11–13. Here, it is evident that Yahweh assigns work that is appropriate in its time. Not only is the timing appropriate, but he has given humanity the ability to contemplate the order and experience the goodness of the earth (verse 12). This is part of the gift God has given to humanity and is part of the assigned tasks and the unchanging rhythms of life (verse 13). This sentiment is echoed in 5:18.[17] This second text also relates the value of eating, drinking, and finding enjoyment in one's work as a gift bestowed from God. Enns rightly states, "Qohelet is correct in taking to heart the pleasures and rewards of life (3:13 and 5:18) and facing the stern reality of death (7:2). These are central components of the human drama for each Israelite, for 'everyone.' But more foundational and central is each Israelite's fear of God and obedience to God's law."[18] The pedagogical tool used for engaging this case is difficult in terms of relating active learning or social cognitive theory. While the author is using literary devices (repetition), in a didactic text that is itself a visual learning tool, this pedagogy falls outside of the established patterns dominantly presented in Wisdom Literature. Though the author is making a significant point relating to religious ethos, it is emphasized through his literary artistry instead of purposefully connecting it to an action or visible reminder. It is unclear from the context why this anomaly exists.

One of the most repeated examples of the integration of nature as a tangible pedagogical tool is the theme of vanity. This is the strongest

17. Enns, *Ecclesiastes*, 10–11.
18. Ibid., 15.

theme of the text, occurring 30 times throughout the book.[19] The word used is הֶבֶל (*hebel*). Rather than "vanity" or "meaningless," this word is better translated as "vapor of breath." It conveys a lack of substance or permanence.[20] The "all" used in connection with this word in verse 2 alludes to the work or activity of humanity. David Hubbard likewise concludes:

> *Hebel* stands more for human inability to grasp the meaning of God's way than for an ultimate emptiness in life. It speaks of human limitation and frustration caused by the vast gap between God's knowledge and power and our relative ignorance and impotence. The deepest issues of lasting profit, of enlightening wisdom, of ability to change life's workings, of confidence that we have grasped the highest happiness—all these are beyond our reach in Koheleth's view.[21]

There are instances where the writer of Ecclesiastes uses this word metaphorically to imply moral incongruity, such as its use in 8:14. However, in other places, it seemingly assumes the literal characteristics of this word and the short lived, ephemeral quality of vapor (*hebel*), as used in 1:2.[22]

It is therefore contended that the writer of Ecclesiastes uses this aspect of nature as a tangible expression to convey his judgment of the fragility of human affairs. It is tirelessly repeated throughout the text to accentuate the dire character of humanity. This is then incorporated as a pedagogical tool that can be tangibly related to by the audience of this text. When the hopeless, fleeting activity of humanity is compared to the eternal state of Yahweh's activity (discussed in Ecclesiastes 3 and 8) the author is able to extrapolate the vastness of Yahweh's activity. Ecclesiastes clearly endorses the limitations of humanity's wisdom. This comparison is another example to support this claim. Humanity is unable to obtain a full comprehension of the wisdom and activity of Yahweh. However, it can become aware of its own limitations and fleeting, empty, activity. Therefore, this tangible knowledge and awareness of self becomes the

---

19. Eccl. 1:14; 2:1, 11, 15, 17, 19, 21, 23, 26; 3:19; 4:4, 7, 8, 16; 5:7, 10; 6:2, 4, 9, 11, 12; 7:6, 15; 8:10, 14; 9:9; 11:8–10; 12:8
20. Harris et al., *TWOT*, 463a.
21. Hubbard, *Ecclesiastes, Song of Solomon*, 48.
22. Davis, *Proverbs, Ecclesiastes, and the Song of Songs*, 167.

pedagogical tool used to better understand, though never fully, the magnitude of Yahweh's eternal activity.

USE OF RELIGIOUS TRADITION IN ECCLESIASTES

The use of religious tradition in Ecclesiastes is directly related to Qoheleth's monologue on his observations and experiences. In his search for life's meaning, Qoheleth uses a blended methodology of both supporting and deconstructing the traditions upheld by his community as he focuses on the individual exceptions to tradition. While he challenges tradition, he ultimately arrives at the consensus view of fearing Yahweh through his argument of remembering the Creator.[23] Because this argument is so readily connected to Creation, the use of religious tradition is discussed more thoroughly later in this chapter in conjunction with the use of the Pentateuch in Ecclesiastes.

PARALLELS WITH THE PENTATEUCH IN ECCLESIASTES

Ecclesiastes incorporates the Pentateuch primarily through its incorporation of Genesis, particularly the emphasis on Creation and the fall of humanity. The discussion of the creation of the heavens and earth first appears in Eccl. 1:2–7 and again in 3:1–8. These sections include Yahweh's personal involvement in Creation as well as the ordering of patterns and seasons. This corresponds to the account of Genesis 1:1–31 as well as 8:22. The acceptance of the formation of man from the dust is recorded in Eccl. 3:20 and reiterated in 12:7. The Genesis counterpart is found in 2:7 as well as 3:19. The Genesis perspective of humanity receiving life through the breath of Yahweh is recorded in Gen. 2:7. Ecclesiastes records this in 12:7. Yahweh's ordination of marriage for a man and woman to enjoy one of life's highest blessings is first described in Gen. 2:18–25. Ecclesiastes affirms this blessing and describes it as a reward of life in Eccl. 9:9. The fallen state of humanity is repeatedly highlighted through Ecclesiastes, as well as Yahweh's judgment for humanity's wickedness. A few examples of this discussion are located in Eccl. 3:14–22; 11:9; 12:14. The fall of humanity is also a prominent theme in Genesis. Its direct discussion is found in 2:17 and 3:1–19. The effect of the fall recurs

23. Bartholomew, *Ecclesiastes*, 87.

throughout Ecclesiastes as the futility of life. One of the earliest examples of this discussion is recorded in Eccl. 1:5–8. Genesis describes the consequences of man's fall in 3:17–19. This passage includes a description of the work that man becomes responsible for as a result of his disobedience to Yahweh's command. Ecclesiastes likewise includes this and reiterates the lack of profit in Eccl. 1:3, 13; 2:3; and 3:9–11. The resulting death of humanity as a consequence of this disobedience is also described in Gen. 2:17 and 3:19. The surety of death for all creatures is repeated throughout Ecclesiastes. Two examples of its discussion include Eccl. 8:8 and 9:4–5. The wickedness of humanity is also continually reiterated throughout Ecclesiastes, such as in 7:20, 29; 8:11 and 9:3. Likewise, Genesis accounts for the wickedness of humanity as a result of disobedience to Yahweh in Gen. 3:22; 6:5; and 8:21. Finally, the withholding of knowledge and wisdom from humanity for unknown reasons is recorded in Gen. 3:22 as well as Eccl. 6:12 and 8:17.

The theology of retribution, based on Deut. 28:1–2, 15, is also confronted in Ecclesiastes. According to the writer of Ecclesiastes, humanity is unable to make sense of the world. Though the writer does not deny the existence of patterns, according to him, sensible patterns and objective goals for nature are elusive to humans.[24] The word he uses for these activities is מַעֲשֶׂה (ma'aseh), such as its use in 8:9. The NASB translates this word as "deed" or "work" in English.[25] Within Ecclesiastes 8, the writer indicates that these deeds are part of the larger "work" (also ma'aseh) of Yahweh.[26] His conclusion, in 8:17, is that humanity cannot discover the connection between the deeds of man and the work of Yahweh. Frustration with this inability to fathom the logistical patterns is repeatedly expressed throughout Ecclesiastes. According to Machinist, "Most significantly, the traditional doctrine of reward and punishment for the good and the wicked does not appear to work, at least in this life."[27] To this end, the author of Ecclesiastes argues against the position of retribution posed in Deuteronomy 28. The chief point made is that the enjoyment of life comes through the acceptance of one's lot in life, distributed by Yahweh. Joy is not obtained by human achievement. The tangible illustration that the writer offers to his audience is that the wicked receive an honor-

---

24. Machinist, "Ecclesiastes," 1603.
25. Harris et al., *TWOT*, 17080a.
26. Eccl. 8:17.
27. Machinist, "Ecclesiastes," 1603.

able burial while the legacy of the righteous is soon forgotten.[28] As he expresses, these are clear exceptions to the theology of retribution. Even the wisest man is unable to fully comprehend Yahweh's ways (*ma'aseh*), and therefore he asserts that humanity must learn to trust Yahweh. This is a position he has emphasized since 6:10.

Examples of active learning that correlate with Fleming's VARK learning theory are present in Ecclesiastes. This can be identified in examples such as its reference to nature through the metaphorical parallel of seeking wisdom as one chases the wind. Ecclesiastes also includes references to Creation such as its descriptions in 1:2–7 and 3:1–8 where readers are told they can learn of Yahweh's involvement and dependability through observing patterns in nature. Similarly to the other books within the Wisdom corpus, Ecclesiastes includes pedagogical examples correlates with the VARK learning theory introduced by Neil Fleming under the larger conceptual framework of active learning theory.

SOCIAL LEARNING THEORY IN ECCLESIASTES

The use of the phrase, "under the sun," is exclusive to Ecclesiastes. It is a broad term that signifies the writer's perspective that the instructions included in this text are for a broader audience than his immediate peers. Instead, it the writer considers his instructions as universal, not connected to a particular time, place, or people.

In addition to establishing a broad audience, Ecclesiastes also establishes a firm expectation for social learning in the first chapter. Immediately, in 1:3, the reader is instructed to consider the preceding generations. They labored and died while the earth remained steadfast. As stated earlier in this chapter, the writer uses this first part of Ecclesiastes 1 to establish that there is no new information conceived. Though younger generations learn from watching their elders, ultimately their labor does not last. History and humanity are eventually forgotten. The value and purpose of life cannot be learned through examples of man's labor, it must come from revelation of the Creator.

Within the text, the writer uses the observations of the main character in association with social cognitive learning. As discussed in chapter 1, social cognitive learning is motivated through communal constructs where behavior is modeled. It was further noted that the

---

28. Deut. 28:10.

vicarious punishment or reward for the observed behavior is assimilated by the learner as if it was personally received. This modeling of behavior becomes a pedagogical model for active learning and is significantly enhanced when the learner can make further inquiries regarding the behavior and outcome. This model for teaching and learning is described in Eccl. 2:18—6:9 as several general observations for the outcome of labor are defined. This pericope begins with an assertion of what happens to the fruit of one's labor and the accumulation of wealth and estate. The writer concludes, in verse 19 that the accrued wealth is eventually lost because the laborer loses his ability to control his wealth after his death. Therefore, the value of labor is brought to question. This conclusion is redirected in verse 26 where the writer asserts that God gives wisdom to those who are obedient. He further asserts that the wealth of the sinner is obstructed and given to the one who is obedient. However, he returns to question the value of labor in Ecclesiastes 3. Here, his observations of social norms lead him to recognize the impermanence of human achievement and human labor. The significance of these observations is the inference that humanity is responsible for discerning the correlation between aligning correct action with the timing and expectations of God. Though God's plan is profound, his timing for each action within his plan is discoverable. To this, Walter Kaiser writes, "This quest is a deep-seated desire, a compulsive drive, because man is made in the image of God to appreciate the beauty of creation (on an aesthetic level); to know the character, composition, and meaning of the world (on an academic and philosophical level); and to discern its purpose and destiny (on a theological level). [. . .] Man has an inborn inquisitiveness and capacity to learn how everything in his experience can be integrated to make a whole."[29] As Qoheleth observes, humanity is incapable of comprehending the value of labor because he cannot "find out the work which God has done from the beginning even to the end."[30] The significance of these social observations and the impact for active learning are important. Within the context of Ecclesiastes 2–3, readers are not instructed to observe the behaviors of others. However, the reader learns of the profound revelation accrued by Qoheleth as a result of his own social observations.

Another observation regarding labor is recorded in Ecclesiastes 4. Here, he offers a conclusion that labor that is based from envy does not

---

29. Kaiser, *Ecclesiastes*, 66.
30. Eccl. 3:11.

produce joy. The word translated as "have seen" is from רָאָה (ra'ah) and is correctly translated as observe or see in the qal tense.[31] Achievement that is the result from the desire for superiority is ultimately self-destructive. The same word is used in verse 7 that follows with the description of seeing a man who labored by himself to accumulate wealth without regard for others. This selfishness is addressed in the text as ambition that does not result in joy. He likewise observes that it is inconsequential to strive for full acceptance by all people. He concludes that power and prestige, like accumulated wealth, does not ultimately result in joy.

Later, in Eccl. 5:1, the reader is instructed to listen while in the house of God. The word translated as "listen" is from שָׁמַע (shama`). It means to hear intelligently and implies obedience to that which is heard.[32] The implication is for the worshipper to enter with an expectation to learn and immediately put into practice the things learned while in the house of God. The pericope closes with the last of a series of nine rephrases of "a chasing after the wind" in Eccl. 6:9.[33] The focus of the full context of 1:14—6:9 is the futility of working with the sole expectation of amassing wealth and prestige. Authority and wealth are both fleeting possessions that are not retained after death. Death is just in its proprietorship of both the rich and the poor, the wise and the fool.

The pedagogical construct of Eccl. 1:14—6:9 is a strong association with social cognitive theory or social learning theory, which is the ability to learn new behaviors (as well as their positive or negative consequences) through observations of others. Here, in this pericope, the social cognitive theory occurs in two layers. The first layer is the author himself who personally observed the behaviors of others and determined what actions are in his best interest for the outcomes he intends. By watching the behaviors modeled by others, he learned which actions and dispositions result in positive reward and which actions and dispositions result in negative consequences. After observing which actions end negatively, he then determines the correct protocol needed to amend the behavior and mindset to gain a positive reward. This leads to the second layer of social cognitive learning as the author then moves to share his information with others. However, he does not solely give instructions, instead, he recounts his observations by recounting the actions and results he observed first

---

31. Harris et al., *TWOT*, 2905.
32. Ibid., 2412.
33. 1:14, 17; 2:11, 17, 26; 4:4, 6, 16.

hand. This is evidenced by the numerous references, "I have seen" and "I saw" each translated from רָאָה (ra'ah).³⁴ The suggestion is that they too learn, not by his instructions, but through the observations of others via testimony of the accounts. Within social cognitive theory, individuals learn new behaviors through the observations of others. This may be reinforced with audible instructions that accompany the modeled behavior.

The next pedagogical feature occurs in Eccl. 9:12. Here, an illustration is made from the trapping of fish and birds. Using both visual and kinesthetic references, the author uses common actions to emphasize his point that misfortune cannot be anticipated. The author then immediately moves back to social cognitive learning theory through the inclusion of his testimony, beginning in verse 13 and again in 10:7. Here, again, the author uses the indicative words, "I have seen" (רָאִיתִי). Following this, he reverts again to visual kinesthetic references in verses 8–11. These four illustrations are used to defend that the value of wisdom in daily activity is negated when not done in the correct timing.

SUMMARY

The polarizing structure of Ecclesiastes is a deliberate literary tension of Hebrew thought that reflects on the paradoxical nature of humanity within the world. The difficulty in interpreting this text is directly related to one's acceptance of Qoheleth's fundamental premise, all earthly action is flawed because of its separation from the divine.³⁵ The closing epilogue brings closure to these tensions by supporting Qoheleth's observations, rather than dismissing them. The long held Israelite ethos of obedience to the law is strongly upheld as the frame narrator brings Qoheleth's observations within the context of retributive theology.

Throughout the text of Ecclesiastes, the author recurrently uses concrete examples for passing on his religious ethos. One of the most repeated examples is the repetitive use of הֶבֶל (hebel). As discussed earlier in this chapter, *hebel* is frequently translated as vanity or meaningless. However, given the overall structure and content of the book, this word conveys a more fundamental premise of quickness or fleeting. This is a strongly developed theme of the text. Life if fleeting and quick; the surety of death exists of all of mankind. The only unknown factor is its timing.

---

34. Cf. Eccl. 1:14; 2:3, 13, 24; 3:10, 16, 22; 4:4, 7, 15; 5:13, 18.
35. Caneday, "Qoheleth," 21.

This use of concrete illustrations is a form of active learning where the learner can associate the properties of what is felt (the fleeting wind) with the properties of what is vague or intangible (the rapidity of life). Additionally, if these concrete examples and illustrations have not been observed by the reader, he or she can likewise investigate and experience them (or reexperience them) as part of the visual and kinesthetic active learning process promoted by Flemming in the VARK learning theory. Finally, these concrete examples remain as ongoing, permanent reminders of the religious instructions associated with them through the Ecclesiastes text.

Another example of active learning occurs in 1:3–7 where the learner is incited to consider the rising and setting of the sun, the cycles of water that fall to earth only to return again. From these examples, the writer asserts that there is nothing permanent and every experience is perpetually in flux. However, it is through the perfection of these cycles in nature that man can begin to conceive of the perfection of eternity. The unseen eternity is witnessed through the observable cycles of nature. He further asserts that Yahweh can be trusted because he is reliable, just as the seasons he created are reliable. In this also, Yahweh is deserving of awe through the flawlessness of his work. Later in the text, the writer goes on to use the unchanging patterns in nature as an example of Yahweh's unchanging plan. Though there are unexpected variables within a single day of nature, the overall season remains consistent. Likewise, the circumstances in one's life may unpredictably change, but the overall pattern and propensity toward Yahweh's ultimate plan remains consistent.

This trust in an overall plan of Yahweh for humanity is a theological conviction strongly held by the Israelites. Here in Ecclesiastes, the writer infuses this religious ideal with a visual pedagogical feature to powerfully relate this ethos through an observable pattern that can be experienced repeatedly as a reminder of this cherished belief.

This connects well with Ecclesiastes 8 where the author uses the word, מַעֲשֶׂה (*ma'aseh*), with a dual purpose. In one context this word is used to describe the tasks or labor of man. Later, it is used as a reference for the work or plan of Yahweh. Here, the writer makes it clear that the amassed, routine tasks or labors of humanity are part of the ultimate plan held by Yahweh. However, the writer has already made it clear that man's labor or work cannot lead to ultimate joy. In an of themselves, they are ambiguous and described as *hebel*, fleeting. Yet, when one learns to trust in Yahweh as a result of understanding the rhythms of nature, he begins to see his own connection to something larger than himself. Thus, every experience in light of the fear of Yahweh leads to unfathomable joy.

However, in this exceptional text, the writer of Ecclesiastes chides the reader as he repeatedly highlights the fallen nature of humanity as a parallel with the teachings in Genesis. As noted in Eccl. 3:14–22; 11:9; 12:14, humanity is limited because of this fallen nature. This leads to boundless frustration that is caused by the vast gap between Yahweh's infinite knowledge and power and exceeding incompetence of humanity that is separated from him. Therefore, a paradox is created within Ecclesiastes. Man must learn by watching and learning from the actions of others but he cannot fully learn from others. Instead, he must be cognizant of Yahweh's activity and learn through the revelation of the Creator.

Second to concrete visual/kinesthetic examples, the use of social cognitive learning theory is a dominant example of pedagogy used in Ecclesiastes. Personal testimony of observations pervades the text. In these examples, the author describes his own experiences and observations as well as the consequences of these events to convey his religious expectations. Rather than merely give instructions and commands on the correct course of action, the writer describes the actions of others and includes the details of the reward or negative result of these actions. This is supported by the multiple uses of רָאָה (ra'ah), "I saw" or "I have seen." Through the use of this pedagogical feature, the writer enables his readers to learn, not by his instructions, but through the eye witness testimony of the observations of others. These visible actions are then reinforced with audible instructions that accompanies observations.

Ecclesiastes includes a variety of pedagogical tools included in Neil Flemming's VARK learning theory. The two most commonly used models are visual and kinesthetic references described through the concrete examples used throughout Ecclesiastes. The second model used social cognitive theory that is used in the author's descriptions of relating himself as a king that allows him to explore through resources uncommon for the common man. He thereby allows his readers to learn through these observations that are not typically available to them.

Reading Ecclesiastes as an inconsequential book that contradicts the rest of the Hebrew Scriptures is a misreading of the text and a conclusion made from poor exegesis. This text is not inconsistent with the Hebrew Bible. Instead, it creates a necessary tension that balances the other texts. It provokes the reader to deeply probe the theological underpinnings and investigate the rationale behind the statements made within the text.

Further, the reader must assimilate and determine how this text fits with the remainder of the Hebrew Bible.

Throughout the teachings of Ecclesiastes, the reader must identify and grapple with the brevity of human life. In this, the reader must also determine his course of actions that allow him to experience either sorrow or great joy. As described in Ecclesiastes, the means for obtaining joy is not through the celebration of man, but in the worship of God. Promotion of one's own plan is grievous but the promotion of God's plan and recognizing one's contribution of work toward the work of God leads to unfathomable enjoyment. These teachings are strikingly consistent with the rest of the Hebrew Bible. Though they are presented in an unorthodox means that may, at times, strike the reader as sacrilegious, they permeate the readers' attention and provoke curiosity. The inquiry of these truths taught in Ecclesiastes can then be explored through the very pedagogical features described in the text. Does one's heart doubt? Then observe and see for yourself where the unknowable is experienced. The experience of the one can be experienced again. There is nothing new under the sun but each experience in creation leads to either the acceptance or denial of the Creator.

Chapter 7

Pedagogy of Song of Songs

PERHAPS AS DIFFERENT AS the subject matter it contains, the pedagogy within the Song of Songs also seduces with its intrigue and dissimilar traits from the other Wisdom texts. Unlike the apparent didactic nature of Job, Proverbs, and Ecclesiastes, the Song of Songs contains no direct reference to teaching or instruction. Likewise, it does not include a reference for watching the social behaviors of others or observing the consequences of disobedience to the religious laws. It bears no reference to fearing God or maintaining the virtuous conduct expected to achieve a respectable social status. Yet, buried within the imagery and euphemistic language exists a strong pedagogical trait that remains consistent with both the experiential and social learning paradigms within the active learning model.

Several pedagogical features are located in Song of Songs that correlate with the conceptual framework for active learning. Specifically, visual and kinesthetic learning are uniquely emphasized through the poetic imagery. The Song of Songs integrates an expectation for innate curiosity and natural inquiry while also addressing social inequity through the literary focus of the text. Unlike other Wisdom texts, Song of Songs does not address the education of children. Here, the focus remains specifically on native adult learners. This is a stark contrast to other texts within the Hebrew Bible. Whereas other biblical Wisdom texts relate pedagogical features through examples of teaching or specific references to teaching social norms, the Song of Songs integrates the use of nature and poetic imagery as a pedagogical resource that encourages experiential learning. While this text does not include a specific reference to religious education nor does it overtly teach a theological doctrine, it does include a distinct affirmation of the active learning model.

Robert Alter correctly describes the poetry of this text as exquisite.[1] He also asserts the grammatical features of the text command a later date for this text, within the post-exilic period.[2] Its poetry includes conspicuous love motifs and celebration of pleasure while also leaving the reader to infer the fear of the Lord. Unlike the poetry of Job and Proverbs, The Song of Songs does not include a sage who guides or advances the readers' attention to a religious ethos or social context of cultic tradition. Here, distinct from other biblical texts, there is no national event, or audible instructions that bring attention instinctively to Yahweh's character or sovereignty.[3] There is no specific mention of covenant, Torah, or Yahweh. Yet, the poetic exchange between two lovers draws in a deeper theological framework amongst perhaps an offensive backdrop of imagery.

The Song of Songs has endured centuries of strained hermeneutical challenges. One of its difficulties is the adult content more suitable for mature readers. Since its content is strikingly different from the rest of the Hebrew Bible, Song of Songs has received several variations in interpretation from literal poetry to allegory. It is beyond the scope of this study to argue and defend a particular hermeneutical style. In accordance with the hermeneutic style already established, the Song of Songs is reviewed through a literary approach to its content. Scholars who use this method of interpretation maintain that its material is comprised of poetry, or collection of love poems,[4] that describe the pinnacle of love experience between two people in a marital relationship, a view readily accepted by early Jewish scholars.[5] The figurative language pervades the whole song. While an indistinct plot is used to propel the "story" forward, identifying an original setting is misplaced with the interpretation of poetry.[6] This exegetical approach for the Song of Songs is accepted by both liberal and conservative scholars[7] as both groups agree that the genre is

1. Alter, *Biblical Poetry*, 231.
2. Alter, *Strong as Death*, §1.
3. Alter, *Biblical Poetry*, 232.
4. Johnston, "The Enigmatic Genre."
5. Hubbard, *Ecclesiastes, Song of Solomon*, 256. This is also evidenced in James MacDonald, "Romantic Love is Exclusive," *Romantic Love: How to Light the Fire and Keep It Burning: Four messages from Song of Solomon*. Walk in the Word (Audio CD) EP650.
6. Hess, *Song of Songs*, 28.
7. See Constable, *Song of Solomon*, 3–4 for a summary of the various views presented.

adapted from Egyptian love poetry.[8] The development of literary analysis advanced the acceptance of its unity and comparison of its techniques to other known poetical styles.[9] A survey of the literature published over the last ten years demonstrates an overwhelming agreement in the acceptance of historical-critical interpretation of the Song of Songs, affirming that its meaning is embedded in the text itself, understood by the original audience, and applicable to modern readers.[10]

Scholars who agree on a literary approach to this text also agree on its explicit nature. Beyond its content, textual criticism reveals the frequency of the feminine voice. Richard Hess also points this out, as well as the remarkable contrast between the celebration of love and love-making recorded in Song of Songs against the brutal descriptions of rape recorded throughout the Hebrew narratives.[11] The Song of Songs enables readers to find balance between the prophets' condemnation of sex in pagan worship and its endorsement within a heterosexual, marital relationship. All five senses are employed in the figurative descriptions that focus on the sexuality of the female and the aesthetics of her body. Once again, this contrasts the male-oriented imagery found elsewhere that often includes sexual descriptions as dry harvest such as Samson's metaphor, "plowed with my heifer," in Judg. 14:18.[12] Here, within the Song of Songs, the focus falls upon the woman who is associated with grace and elegance.[13] She is endowed with power, an anomaly for the status of women in the Hebrew Bible.[14] According to Hess, "The effect of this imagery is to provide the

---

8. Further analysis of the form, structure, and historical context is discussed in the introduction of Ariel Bloch and Chana Bloch, trans., *The Song of Songs: The World's First Great Love Poem*.

9. Hess, *Song of Songs*, 25, 27.

10. A few examples of this acceptance is found in Robert Alter's afterword published in Bloch's, *The Song of Songs* (2006), G. Loyd Carr, *The Song of Songs* (2009), Richard Hess, *The Song of Songs* (2005).

11. Hess, *Song of Songs*, 35. Hess does not include examples of such accounts. Readers may be drawn to narratives such as Gen. 34; Judg. 19:22–28; Judg. 21:10–23; or 2 Sam. 13:1–22.

12. Hess, *Song of Songs*, 29.

13. Consider her description in terms of doves, 2:12; 6:9, gazelles 4:5; 7:3, and flowers 2:1.

14. Consider the woman's simile of a mare let out among the Pharaoh's chariots in 1:9.

female with the tools necessary to control her destiny and thus to choose her lover even as he chooses her."[15]

J.P. Fokkelman rightly states, "Sensitivity to verse has something to do with aptitude, and a lot to do with proper training."[16] Reading biblical poetry requires the reader to have competence and experience in the linguistic tools utilized by the writer. The richness and meaning of the text is portrayed in relatively few words. Yet, word studies do not necessarily yield as much theological insight as they do for narrative texts because meaning is derived mainly from the whole of the image rather than the accuracy of the word.[17] The vastness of the imagery gives density and complexity through carefully selected words that probe the imagination while also remaining securely focused on the rhythmic portrayal of events and soulful emotion.[18] The Song of Songs uses both sight and sound enjoyed by the couple to bring the reader into the experiences of the account. The seductive tones of the refrain, "My beloved is mine and I am his," offer an alliteration of vowel sounds in the Hebrew text. Fokkelman summarizes this literary phenomenon as he writes, "In a combination with the word meanings these vowels form a chiasm, as the perfect expression of reciprocity: the two belong to each other heart and soul. The closed-ness of the AB-B1A1 pattern symbolizes their inseparability."[19]

The interpreter does well to pay close attention to the parallelism, alliteration, and rhythmic sounds of an oral reading of the poetry. Moreover, the reader must demonstrate restraint by not assigning more meaning to individual terms than the context allows. The imagery calls for imagination while the biblical text demands restraint and conviction in its interpretation.

---

15. Hess, *Song of Songs*, 30.

16. Fokkelman, *Reading Biblical Poetry*, 15.

17. This is not to say that the words are trivial or unimportant. As previously stated, poetry is meticulous in the selection of words. Instead, the meaning is derived more fully from the image, not a single word within the imagery.

18. Fokkelman, *Reading Biblical Poetry*, 15.

19. Ibid., 195.

USE OF NATURE

The Song of Songs portrays life from conception[20] to death.[21] Peter van der Zwan argues that nature may play just as vital role as the lovers; it is personified and depicted as alive.[22] The garden metaphor is one of the dominate themes throughout the song where vegetation is used figuratively to express eroticism and fertility that is masked in literary discretion. The eruptive use of fruits, spices, florals, and fragrances ensures the imagery references are not lost on its readers. The direct association of these references was common practice in figurative writing. The sights and smells underlying these images present a sensory conduit of attraction.[23] The enclosed garden offers an interesting contrast between nature and humanity. As Patrick Hunt points out, flowers do not have secrets of their own to hide but may be used to hide the secrets of others.[24] This wooded paradise garden offers a place of union and a literary masterpiece that cultivates the readers' senses for experiencing the lucid love affair alongside the characters.

The Song of Songs endorses an exclusivity of love. The couple's love is as intense at the beginning as the end, a love longed for when apart. It is a love reserved exclusively for the covenant partner.[25] It is a love as strong as death, freely given, yet beyond price.[26] The Christian Canon uses marital love as a basis for understanding divine love.[27] It is thus proposed that a biblical book was inspired to offer a prototype of authentic love between a man and a woman.

> Sexual love provides many people with their first experience of ecstasy, which literally means 'standing outside oneself.' Therefore, the experience of healthy sexual desire can help us imagine what it might mean to love God truly [. . .] Like the love of God, profound love of another person entails devotion of the whole self and steady practice of repentance and forgiveness; it inevitably requires of us suffering and sacrifice.[28]

20. SOS 3:4.
21. SOS 8:6.
22. Van der Zwan, "Song of Songs," 1.
23. Hunt, *Poetry in the Song*, 105.
24. Ibid., 106.
25. SOS 2:16, 6:3, 7:10.
26. SOS 8:6.
27. cf. Lev. 19:18; Matt. 22:36–39; John 13:34–35.
28. Davis, *Proverbs, Ecclesiastes, and the Song of Songs*, 233.

Within the repeating themes of this poetry, begins a loosely interwoven plot of a young couple who yearn for one another. Nearly unable to abstain from sex until their wedding night, they obsess for one another. Erotic, sensual love is graphically described between the lovers. As their wedding night arrives, the two finally come together unhindered in the consummation of their new covenant with one another. Yet, as the song continues, the couple does not always rejoice in such bliss as arguments befall their marriage and the lovers struggle to express their love. Yet, the end provides the reader with the impression that the two lovers rejoin. Though their marriage has now experienced the trials of time, it is no less erotic than the early romance of the days of their youth, awaiting their nuptials.[29] The Song of Songs describes the perfection of marital love that includes trials and misunderstandings between lovers. Yet, the love that is only acquired through age and time together is no less sensual and worthy of longing for than the anticipation of the first sexual touch upon one's body. Within the overall biblical context, physical love in Song of Songs is cast as positive and contrasts with the negative statements on adultery and promiscuity found in other Wisdom texts.[30] As Hess explains, "Sex plays a secondary role to desire."[31] The repetitive use of love (אַהֲבָה, 'ahăbâ),[32] refers to loyalty, a clear commitment to the covenantal love agreed upon by both parties. Consider its use in texts such as Song of Sol. 2:4, "His banner over me is love" and Song of Sol. 8:6, "love is as strong as death." The Song does not recognize a dichotomy between the personal relationship and the physicality of sex when describing the consummation of their love.[33]

A reexamination the pedagogical function of Song of Songs demonstrates its use similarly to the didactic nature of narrative accounts. Stern articulates, "Although the Song of Songs was not written by a single author as a narrative whole, the various poetic devices—including verbatim repetitions, recurring genres, and thematic echoes—encourage it to be read as an unfolding story."[34] The continuity of scenes, refrains, and po-

---

29. Consider the parallel verses of 2:24, 17 and 8:13–14. In both cases, the male calls for his maiden and asks to hear her voice. In both of her responses, she beckons him to hurry to her; the purpose of his haste is to enjoy the sensuality of her body.

30. Hess, *Song of Songs*, 33.

31. Ibid., 32.

32. Harris et al., *TWOT*, 29c.

33. Hess, *Song of Songs*, 33.

34. Stern, "Song of Songs," 1566.

etic imagery achieves a powerful description that is intended to be read and interpreted as a unified collection. Its impact remains in the context of engaging the entire text with its central theme. The Song of Songs offers an impressive affirmation of an enduring intimate relationship. The canonicity of this literature joins together the genuine intimacy of human contact with the sacredness of Yahweh.

Within the narrative accounts, right and wrong action is not always made explicitly clear. Instead, the readers must infer correct behavior based on the trajectory of the account and either the blessings or lack thereof that ensue. Similarly, the Song of Songs does not insert its own conclusion regarding the behaviors of the couple. However, readers are also devoid of a larger metanarrative that allows for a greater context beyond the immediate "story." Therefore, the interpretation and full meaning is found only within the song itself.[35] As in the narratives, readers must create their own conclusion regarding right and wrong. Yet, even more important, readers must also conclude how the Song of Songs relates to God and its relevance to the Hebrew Bible.

The use of nature as a pedagogical tool is an ongoing phenomenon within the Hebrew Bible. However, in other contexts, it is most often used as a memorial as observed in the stacking of stones or pillars described in the Pentateuch and Deuteronomistic History.[36] Nature is also used as a reminder, such as the sign of the rainbow to trigger the memory of Yahweh's covenant in Genesis 17. Within Wisdom Literature, nature is used to point to more grand objectives and patterns such as the use of the planning of the insects to relate to social decorum[37] or the changing of the seasons to illustrate Yahweh's providential governance and reliability.[38] Yet, within the Song of Songs, it is difficult to ascertain the role of nature and a pedagogical feature. It is not described as a memorial or a reminder. Neither are readers instructed to view it as a specific transference of patterns to better relate to Yahweh. Moreover, given its emphatic association within the Song, any strong transfer of characteristics to Yahweh leaves the interpreter with horrific theological implications. Thus again, the reader is left with a biblical book that is, perhaps, in a category unique to

---

35. I would, however, certainly argue for the greater context of the Hebrew Canon.
36. See Gen. 28:18–22 and Josh. 4:7 as examples.
37. Prov. 10:5.
38. Eccl. 3:1–11.

itself. While the Song of Songs is correctly defined as Wisdom Literature, its specific use of nature is unlike that of the other Wisdom texts.

Nature maintains its role as a pedagogical tool used for religious instruction, within the context of the Song of Songs. However, its use is strikingly different from the other Wisdom texts. Here, instead of pointing directly to Yahweh's attributes, it is used to invoke the senses of the reader. Its role is to engulf the reader in such a way that the emotion is recreated, allowing the reader to personally experience the full spectrum of emotions portrayed throughout the Song. The longing, the arousal, the ecstasy, the hurt, and the joy are all repeatedly experienced firsthand. While different, it is a similar use to that found in the narratives.

Within the narrative accounts, a generation of people personally experience a direct action of Yahweh. Thus, they memorialized the event through the naming of the area, the stacking of stones, or integrating it into their religious festivals. This then provoked curiosity from those lacking association with the original event and thus allow the story teller to relate the event through descriptions that likely engrossed the listener, allowing the experience to be relived. Likewise, the Song of Songs allows the readers to relive the events portrayed. Though the paradigm has shifted, the primary role of a previous generation "telling an account" to a newer generation is a long engrained tradition for the Israelite culture. Here within the Song of Songs, nature remains a pedagogical tool. However, it is not a memorial or used as a transference of characteristics. Instead, it is the vehicle itself in which the writers used to invoke experiential learning. Here, the learner is not actively touching or seeing. Instead, it is a combination and direct association of emotion and sensory memory.

The religious ethos of the community of believers concludes a deep relationship between Yahweh and his covenant people. It is a relationship often described in the deep relationship of choice between spouses. Therefore, it is plausible that the Song of Songs is used, not only as a prototype for affectionate love but also as a model. Within the fallen humanity as well as the cultural variances that skew the defining characteristics of love (אַהֲבָה, 'ahăbâ), it is possible that the word fluctuates in resonance from person to person, based on experience. Therefore, an architype is created. However, in keeping with expectation, it is not merely described, but written so that it may be experienced.

USE OF TRADITION

As it is an anomaly in its use of nature, the Song of Songs is also an anomaly to the Hebrew Bible as it relates to the use of tradition and references to religious heritage. Due to its specific content and purpose, it does not use the traditional references of major events from Israel's past experiences. Alternatively, it tends to go against expected stereotypes that were normative in the social decorum of its original setting. As stated earlier, the anticipated use of the male character as the dominate voice and role for the text is not followed. Instead, it is the female character who is empowered and described as radiant and desired.

This poetry also engages the reader in a style atypical of similar literature. Within biblical poetry, the audience is implied and often identifies as a masculine figure or character. The dominant pattern is a male central speaker, with whom the audience identifies as "self." However, within the Song of Songs, the principle speaker is feminine and encourages the reader's immediate identification with the feminine character. The female character is empowered from the first verse of the text as she speaks first, forcefully, and sensually. This is an abrupt contrast to other biblical texts that readily portray women in a lower social group then men. As property of her father and later her husband, it is inconceivable to characterize the female character in the manner in which she is empowered as noted in the Song of Songs. It is likely this depiction and absence of narration would produce an immediate tension and disequilibrium for the reader as it goes against the cultural expectation for social decorum.

PARALLELS WITH THE PENTATEUCH

Daniel Estes accurately reflects this song's example of pedagogy. "Instead of merely reporting the experience of the characters, the book, as poetry, endeavors to re-create their experience in the reader."[39] As previously stated, all five senses are stimulated, through the range of poetic images, to elicit an emotional response from the reader. Estes further states, "The reader must enter imaginatively into the literary world of the author."[40] The senses are used in the process of religious education. Whereas the narratives primarily engaged vision and touch, the Song of Songs engages

---

39. Estes, *Handbook on the Wisdom*, 401.

40. Ibid., 402.

the senses through its use of metaphors and phonological features in its recreation of physical experiences. It does not offer the tangible memorial or locations, as demonstrated in the Deuteronomistic History. Instead, it relies on the experiential learning more aptly aligned with the examples established in Deuteronomy.

The sacrificial, covenant love espoused in the repeated word אַהֲבָה ('ahăbâ) throughout the Song of Songs, is a clear commitment the lovers make to one another. This is a divergence from the Hebrew narratives where covenantal love is depicted between Yahweh and humanity, as observed in Deut. 7:8. Like Song of Songs, Deuteronomy depicts the covenantal love between God and man through emotions. Yet, in the narratives, it is God who loves Israel with this sacrificial love. Interestingly, throughout the entirety of the Hebrew Bible, אַהֲבָה is used to describe either God's love for humanity or love between two humans. This deeply seeded love (אַהֲבָה) is not used as a description for humanity's love for Yahweh.

Though physical love is the focus of Song of Songs, Hess explains this love is not unlike the love for God that the community of faith experiences as it joins with God in fulfillment of its mission.[41] This love, as strong as death, is not derivative of human emotion. To this, Hess writes:

> [It] demonstrates the power of those parts of our being that can lie on the very edge of full encounter with God. Love for God here transcends covenantal fidelity alone and achieves an arousal and joy that is never consummated fully in this life. The saints of Christianity sometimes understood this, and so for them there was no discontinuity between the Song and the passion for God. These two expressions of desire welled up from the same center of their being. For them, then, it became the closest experience this side of the grave of the transcendent knowledge of the living God. As passion was a shortcut to knowing God in this life, so death itself became the door to that eternal knowledge.[42]

The commitment of this love culminates in SOS 8:6-7 where it is described as a force not otherwise known and potentially lays the groundwork for the LXX Greek rendering of אַהֲבָה as ἀγάπη (*agápē*). This love, as strong as death, is experienced through two individuals passionately seeking after one another. It is the same enthusiasm Hosea uses to

---

41. Hess, *Song of Songs*, 33.
42. Ibid., 33-34.

describe God's pursuit of and commitment to humanity.[43] It is Hess who points out, the one-for-one correlation throughout the Song between the eleven appearances of the word for love (אַהֲבָה) in the Hebrew text and the LXX as ἀγάπη.[44] It is here, that perhaps the pedagogical value of the Song of Songs begins to reveal itself.

SUMMARY

All five senses are activated in the sensory imagery of Song of Songs. Robert Alter notes the combination of multiple senses into a single image to enrich the senses even further.[45] This is observable in 4:10 where love is described in the taste of wine and fragrance of oil. The image continues in 4:11 with the focus intensifying on the woman whose lips are described in the taste of honey and milk while her garments smell of Lebanon. Here both taste and smell are combined to strengthen the readers' arousal. Another example is found in 1:7 where three senses are utilized in a single reference. Here, sight, taste, and touch are all applied. Alter goes on to assert that the sensory characteristics are frequently grouped in two pairs, sight with sound, and taste with smell that are combined to create the sensory experience.[46] Thus, active learning is introduced, not necessarily as a direct model addressed but rather as an indirect association the readers gain by experiencing the emotions portrayed throughout the text and creating their own connotation for relating this biblical text with the rest of the Hebrew Bible. Hunt rightly expresses, "[These] multiple sensory clusters greatly enhance the memorable qualities of the figures and makes them all the more facile to imagine and remember by experiential association with not just one sensory memory but interconnected memory."[47]

The audacity that Yahweh loves his people is nearly unfathomable. In a circumvention of misguided definitions of this love, an example is set forth in the Song of Songs. Unlike other texts within the Hebrew Bible, where readers can observe specific references to educating the youth or specific examples of religious education taking place, the nature of Song of Songs demands more attention. Though it is comprised of a series of

---

43. Hos. 11:8 9.
44. Hess, *Song of Songs*, 250.
45. Alter, *Biblical Poetry*, 202.
46. Ibid., 211.
47. Hunt, *Poetry*, 85.

poems, dismantling the text into brief pericopes devalues the overall message of the text as a unified whole. It is only in its entirety that the reader learns (or is reminded) of an important facet of love. Love, as depicted in this Song, is beyond measure. It cannot be fully explained, only experienced. Likewise, it is here in the strongest of bonds, that humanity gets a glimpse into the immeasurable love Yahweh has for his people. It is a love that knows no bounds. It too, cannot be fully explained, only experienced. Consequently, God is love. To know him, one must know love. Yet, it is submitted that not every person finds this deepest of human bonds. Through the fallen nature of humanity, love becomes subjected to distorted human objectivity. Therefore, embedded in the biblical text, is a book that allows the reader to engage all his or her senses in a journey of passion between lovers, where love knows no boundaries. The purest sense of love and physical passion brings both heartache and the greatest of pleasure. The disciplined obedience taught in the Torah is juxtaposed with the freedom of pleasure anticipated in the Song of Songs and the celebration of unconditional, experiential love. Used in conjunction with the Hebrew Bible, the entire text of Song of Songs becomes a pedagogical resource in and of itself that allows the reader to enter in to the community of faith and begin to engage in the ethos of a God who relentlessly pursues humanity.[48] Here, love is not described; it is experienced.

Song of Songs does not directly relate its text to the relationship of humanity and Yahweh, nor should it be allegorically interpreted as such. Instead, it is fundamentally a series of poems that contribute to an overall depiction of human love that is brilliantly depicted through unmatched imagery allowing the reader to experience the emotions firsthand. This model of active learning is a literary achievement that strongly bonds the use of both sensory active learning and social cognitive learning through the characters. This text then, becomes a basis for assimilating the illustrations of Yahweh's depiction of love for humanity with the emotion learned through the illustration of love through the pedagogy related in Song of Songs. It is active learning in order to experience what one can only learn through involvement. Through this text, the reader's imagination is provoked to curiosity through the intensity of sensual imagery and the unimaginable becomes real.

---

48. By stating this, I do not intend to disengage from the literary approach to this text nor do I, in any means, move toward allegorizing the text. Instead, the love associated with the Song of Solomon becomes the gauge for understanding the love of God described in other biblical texts.

Chapter 8

Summary

THE OBJECTIVE OF THIS study is to investigate the pedagogical features represented within Wisdom Literature. This has entailed a survey of the final canonical forms of Job, Proverbs, Ecclesiastes, and Song of Songs for pedagogical features described in each of these texts. In conclusion of the research presented, it is argued that the final forms of the Wisdoms texts included in the Hebrew Bible contain strong examples of active learning through visual, kinesthetic and social cognitive learning.

Wisdom Literature, within the Hebrew Bible, is written to "evoke a world charged with God's grandeur as the Creator and redeemer."[1] It summons the readers to live their lives conscious of Yahweh's expectations described within his laws. It uses the aesthetic nuances of poetry to cajole, if not command readers to comply with their religious obligations. Bartholomew and O'Dowd state, "Its creativity with words, sounds and images gives it its evocative and memorable powers."[2] The Wisdom corpus is then integrated into the daily affairs of homes and religious practices of the community where it generates a "formative presence in the cultural consciousness of God's people."[3]

Wisdom Literature uses specific events as reminders of religious ideals concerning the characteristics and worship of Yahweh. Other texts, such as Proverbs and Job, lean on other observations as a means of transferring knowledge. Not only is the learner required to observe the behaviors and

1. Bartholomew and O'Dowd, *Old Testament Wisdom Literature*, 58.
2. Ibid.
3. Ibid.

consequences of others, but observations from nature are used to further educate the learner with religious concepts. "In addition to observing the physical world, wisdom also observes and learns from the full range of human activities. Assuming that human nature is more or less a constant, wisdom uses what it sees in the lives of people to develop lessons for constructive behavior."[4] While this is a variance from the pedagogy illustrated in the Pentateuch and Deuteronomistic History, the commonality is the maintained use of tangible objects as pedagogical tools of religious education. Daniel Estes speaks to this as he discusses Proverbs and writes, "It is evident that the learner is counseled to make literal observations of the actions of the animal."[5] These observations are then directly related to the religious ideals the teacher seeks to convey to the learner.

Wisdom Literature addresses the means by which those who adhere to Yahweh must live in accordance with social and religious obligations. Alongside this, it addresses the anomalies that seemingly do not align with the laws described in the Pentateuch, specifically retributive theology. Like the Pentateuch and Deuteronomistic History, Wisdom Literature illustrates the importance of obedience to Yahweh's laws through relating kinesthetic and visual instructional aids (such as history and nature) to assist the learners of grasping the religious ethos of the instructor.

EXPLORATION OF THE RESEARCH QUESTIONS

If a community is to survive, it must concern itself with the education of its youth. It must prepare younger generations for future responsibilities and the expected social constructions of skills, information, rules of conduct, and religious ethos. In preparation for answering the research question regarding the types of pedagogy included in Wisdom Literature, chapter 1 presented the background for informal education and the descriptions of pedagogy and learning theories.

As presented in chapter 1, education continues to develop and adapt. Though cultures and generations impact educational trends, the fundamental premise of communicating information from an instructor to a learner remains unchanged. Education involves the entire process of transmitting this information of accumulated knowledge, mythos, and ethos from one generation to the next within a community.

4. Estes, 90.
5. Ibid.

Within education is pedagogy, the means by which this information is communicated. It calls on the imagination of both the instructor and the learner to create both the environment and vehicle by which information is shared and received. This imagination reshapes experiences to emphasize or reinforce the facts not present within the context of a present learning setting. It allows the learner to move past the boundaries of the immediate setting to a place of inquiry and authentic learning. Studies support that children learn through both physical and imagined experiences. As stated earlier, this imaginative narrative allows the learner to create what does not exist and practice observed behaviors in a safe place. They further support that the process of imagination has great value in the learning process as it triggers many of the same brain functions as real experiences. Therefore, it is postulated that a learner can learn vicariously through active imagination that is activated through testimony in much the same way as experiencing the story firsthand.

Truth is constructed through both personal experience and social paradigms created through testimony. Social interactions readily create informal educational settings through the interactions that take place and oral dialogues exchanged between individuals. These shared experiences and social interactions provide learners with informal education in areas such as social expectations, cultural heritage, and religious practices.[6]

Highly supported in education is the role of active learning that emphasizes the learner's knowledge acquisition through sensory experiences. The combination of any of the five senses with auditory instructions (regardless of age) greatly impacts memory retention over audible instructions that is not accompanied with any other sense. This active/experiential learning is achieved as the learner physically participates through touch, sight, activity or inquiry. This type of learning activates several areas of the brain making learning more meaningful.

Also discussed in chapter 1 is the ongoing research in mirror neurons that create meaningful learning and long-term memory through both physical activity and observation of the same activity. The learning acquired from observation of human behavior creates deep meaningful learning that is indiscriminate from learning firsthand.[7] Behavior observation and mimicry create lifelong patterns of behavior in the learner. It is further attested that the brain responds the same way regardless of

---

6. Pazimiño, *Foundational Issues*, 84.
7. Bandura. *Social Foundations*.

whether an experience is real or imagined. Otherwise stated, the brain does not differentiate between learning through a physical experience or learning through the observation of someone's else's behavior. In either case, the learner responds and learns.

It is through experiences that learners accommodate or assimilate information. Yet, learners can obtain the same active learning patterns through personal experience as well as the observation of the experiences of others. By experiences and observation of social patterns and positive or negative consequences that result from actions, learners are able to critically examine and question social norms to evaluate their value and need for continuation. Learning theorists agree that learners acquire knowledge in a variety of ways. The dominate means for learning and memory retention is active learning that involves two or more senses.

Within Wisdom Literature, there is substantial evidence to support the use of active learning through the interaction of the faith community and inclusion of concrete examples of visual and kinesthetic illustrations that reinforce the instructions included in the texts. It also utilizes social cognitive learning patterns. As discussed in chapter 1, Jeanne Omrade concludes, "[the] social cognitive theory focuses on what and how people learn from one another, encompassing such concepts as observational learning, imitation, and modeling."[8] This social interaction is an important means for learning cultural expectations through the modeling of behavior that is combined with inquiry and instruction. Learning is further motivated through these social interactions and the observation of punishment and reward for specific behaviors.[9] This positive and negative reinforcement of behavior is a fundamental requirement for the vicarious learning of modeled behavior. As observed in Wisdom Literature, informal education takes place in the social contexts described in the biblical texts.

Finally, chapter 1 summarized that behavior is not only learned through trial and error of one's own actions, but learners can acquire the same experiential learning vicariously through the observation of the actions of others in a social community. More importantly, learners learn through observing the consequences of these behaviors.[10] The positive or negative reinforcement of these behaviors directly impacts the

---

8. Ormrod, *Human Learning*, 118.
9. Gage and Berliner, *Educational Psychology*, 340.
10. Ormrod, *Human Learning*, 119.

likelihood of whether or not the observer will repeat the same actions.[11] Furthermore, the observation of behaviors facilities the swifter learning and desired future patterns of behavior from the learner than personally experiencing the behaviors firsthand.

The research questions are also explored using a literary approach to the biblical texts. chapter 2 discussed various approaches biblical study and defended the use of a literary approach as the most conducive method for adequately exploring the pedagogical features included in the Wisdom texts. Additionally, this chapter summarized some of the prevalent definitions for wisdom and narrowed the focus of defining wisdom as both character and literature.

The existence of editorial activity within Wisdom Literature is widely accepted among scholars. The transmission of sayings by elders is maintained as a social discipline within the community. The memory of these oral sayings is passed from one generation to the next until it is recorded at a later point in history. The appropriation of borrowed material is reimagined through the Yahwistic faith and contextualized as a means for further addressing the social expectations of the faith community. As the wisdom traditions are recorded, the writers and editors include concrete illustrations to further clarify the instructions and perspectives contained within the account. They also include descriptions of personal observations or testimony that furthers anchors the "story" or religious mythos/ethos that is represented in a specific context. In additional to their cultural expectations that are espoused in their religious traditions, the writers and editors preserved their teaching techniques (or pedagogy) as an example for replicating similar techniques as the traditions continue to be preserved and retaught. This important feature of literary artistry is used in the subsequent chapters where examples of pedagogy are defended.

Because of the didactic nature of Wisdom Literature and the intrinsic focus on the education of youth, chapter 3 offers a description of the construction of childhood as represented in the Hebrew Bible. As an emerging field in biblical research, the existing body of knowledge is underdeveloped in comparison to the substantial studies in other social norms relating to biblical literature. However, the defining characteristics of childhood are guided by the social interactions that govern them. This directly relates to the elder members' determination of the value of

---

11. Ibid., 127.

education for those younger than themselves. As discussed in chapter 3, increasing the education of the child has a direct correlation of not only raising the value of the child but also is regarded as directly associated with ensuring the community's survival. Guided by the instructions of the Torah, the Nation of Israel regards obedience to the religious laws as the determining factor impacting Yahweh's blessing and protection for them. They therefore emphatically support the importance of educating the younger generations to avoid replicating the unfortunate failure exemplified in Jdgs. 2:10–12, a generation who was left uninformed of their religious heritage and obligation.

Chapters 4–7 directly relate to the research question concerning the types of pedagogical features that are described in Wisdom Literature. These chapters surveyed the literature contained in the final form of the Wisdom corpus to show that it includes descriptions of pedagogy that are consistent with modern studies in active and social cognitive learning. Evidence of active learning through visual and kinesthetic experiences is repeatedly recorded throughout these texts. There are a variety of pedagogical features described within Wisdom Literature; however, the dominant use is the witness of nature for Yahweh. Examples of this are located in Job 12:7–8, Prov. 10:5; 26:2, and Ecc. 3:11–33 and the use of social cognitive learning that is further discussed below.

The use of nature, tradition, Pentateuch, and social contexts are also explored in chapters 4–7. While examples of active learning that correlate with Flemings VARK learning theory are present in Job, specific references to teaching or instructional methods are minimal. However, the author strongly incorporates nature as a visual and kinesthetic agent for teaching the characteristics of Yahweh.

Recorded in Job 12, readers are informed that the agents through which learners gain insight into Yahweh's character are the animals he created, namely beasts, birds, and fish. Within the context, Job speaks to Bildad stating that the world and retributive theology does not operate the way his friends have argued. He calls for the witness of nature in order to support his hypothesis. Later, in Job 38–41, it is likewise nature that Yahweh uses in his response to Job's accusations of injustice. Yahweh's providential control of nature is illustrated along with the diminutiveness of Job and humanity. The overall message is that wisdom is found only in Yahweh who allocates it to humanity as he determines appropriate. The subtle reminders for this object lesson are found in the sun, sea, ox, and steed. This tangibility of nature allows Job to transfer his experiences from nature to the intangible character of Yahweh. While the illustration is directed to Job, these examples are vicariously set as reminders for the readers of Job who may likewise use these tangible objects for their own active learning and recognition of wisdom through God.

Within the text of Job, Yahweh himself engages as an instructor. In one of the most robust examples of Yahweh's direct address and instruction, his use of concrete examples and active learning is unmistakable. Yahweh's supremacy is intangible. He therefore associates it with things Job can see and experience, allowing him to make a direct correlation between the two. Job's friends, on the other hand, use Israelite tradition as a means for relating their religious ethos. Yet, the prudent instructions of Eliphaz likewise use nature, specifically creation, to warn Job of the consequences of his theological insurgence. However, the writer clearly brings focus to the instruction method of Yahweh through the inclusion of the statement, "Who teaches like God?" It is Yahweh's instructions to Job that are central to his transformation. The concrete examples of nature are used for support of his assertion of sovereign control.

Yet, it is the illustration of social cognitive learning embodied in the entire book of Job that is perhaps the most astounding. As related in chapter 4, Job's character allows for the observation of behavior and their consequences by the reader. Directly relating to Dewey's philosophy of imagination in education and the substantive studies in mirror neurons that assert learning is facilitated through observation and imagination just as strongly as if it was personally experienced. By identifying with Job's character, the reader has the ability to construct a reality that likewise affirms the recognition of Yahweh's supremacy and justice.

Just as Job is transformed through the concrete examples and active learning used by Yahweh, so the reader can associate Job's experience through the observations of his patterns of behavior and the direct correlation of the trajectory of events that ensue from his declarations. Job learns that though he cannot see Yahweh, the effects of Yahweh's control of nature and humanity are undeniable. Thus, the tangibility of nature is a kinesthetic and visual tool for teaching the invisible characteristics of Yahweh. Through the descriptions of events, readers are likewise enabled to learn from the actions of the characters. They too, experience the emotions portrayed in the text and substantiate whether their similar patterns of thinking place them in a similar trajectory of self-destruction. In imagining themselves in the story, they vicariously learn and transform alongside Job.

Summary

Similarly to the of social cognitive learning gained through observing the character of Job, the son described in Proverbs, is instructed to observe human behavior in the physical world in order to gain insight in the behaviors that merit punishment and reward.

Prov. 10:5 endorses the use of nature. Here the ant is referenced as a pedagogical feature to relate social decorum. Once again, nature is the resource that humanity may observe to draw conclusions on how to conduct behavior in accordance with religious laws. Here, the insignificant ant demonstrates the social expectation of working hard during harvest so that it can maintain life when food is scarce. Presently, there is no existing study that challenges the visual imagery within Proverbs. The repetition of metaphor, such as the reoccurring role of the two paths, connects a concrete example with instruction thus moving the methodology from passive to active learning.

More importantly, the voice of Wisdom in Prov. 8:22–31 includes a personification that allows readers to "rediscover" Yahweh as Creator through the observations of his interaction with creation. Similar to the illustrations from Job, the intangibility of Yahweh is overcome by the tangible experiences and transference of knowledge from the effects of Yahweh in nature to the supremacy of his character. The tangibility of everyday experiences in nature are permeated with the governing providence of Yahweh. Thus, experiencing creation is a means for experiencing God.

Likewise, Ecclesiastes also draws on nature as the writer expresses confidence in Yahweh's providential care. Within Ecclesiastes, more concrete examples for relating theological instructions are provided than any of the other Wisdom texts. In addition to this pattern for visual and kinesthetic learning, a pattern for social cognitive learning is also strongly reinforced through the testimony of Qoheleth's personal observations. These are further reinforced by his inclusion of the positive and negative consequences for these behaviors.

The reliability of the changing seasons is used as an illustration for Yahweh's perfected oversight over creation and thus the evidence to what cannot be observed within eternity. Humanity learns to trust Yahweh through the reliability of the seasons[12] and learns to fear Yahweh through the flawlessness of his work. Like Job and Proverbs, Ecclesiastes draws from observations and patterns in creation as evidence for the perfection of the Creator.

12. Eccl. 3:1–11.

In Ecclesiastes 11, it is contended that humanity cannot fathom the full plans of Yahweh. However, the overall unchanging rhythms of nature point to the unchanging character of Yahweh. The paradox of Ecclesiastes is man's search for meaning but inability to find it. Here, the religious ethos of trusting in Yahweh's sovereign providence is powerfully related through the connection of humanity's minuscule toils in the magnificent works of Yahweh. While humanity is fleeting, Yahweh is eternal. Humanity is small and ignorant in comparison to the grandeur and infinite expertise of Yahweh. The concrete examples included in Ecclesiastes strongly relate the purpose of man is not to labor and achieve in order to further honor himself, but to recognize his role in the plans constructed by Yahweh. Similar to the proposition for son to observe the behaviors of others in Proverbs, Ecclesiastes models the wisdom gained by watching the actions of others. By watching these behaviors, Qoheleth learns the consequences of both obedience and disobedience to the religious laws.

Finally, chapter 7 relates the active learning models observable in the Song of Songs. While this book is a stark contrast in its subject matter from the other Wisdom texts, it too includes strong examples of active learning. Specifically, it incorporates multiple senses in its imagery that pulls the reader into the "story." This combination of senses enriches the imagery. As observed in 4:10–11, imagery activating the senses for taste and smell are combined to strengthen the reader's arousal. The effect is the readers' vicarious experiences of the emotions and social learning associated through the imagination that is provoked through the layers of imagery included in the text. In a circumvention of the misguided notions of love, the Song of Songs portrays authentic pattern for love that is untainted from fallacy. It is here that readers gain a perspective that goes on to guide them as they read other biblical texts that relate Yahweh's love for humanity. A love that knows is immeasurable, knows no bounds, and is as strong as death.

ASSESSMENT OF THIS RESEARCH METHODOLOGY

The original research questions guiding the research are answered and supported. Wisdom Literature incorporates examples of visual imagery, tangible examples, and social cognitive learning in the religious education of faith adherents. These teaching techniques are sub-theories under the larger conceptual framework of active learning. The strongest examples of these include observations of nature (visual and kinesthetic), and observations of others (social cognitive).

The Wisdom corpus incorporates specific examples of pedagogy into its texts. While there are some similarities of testimonies and locations used, Wisdom integrates nature as its dominant pedagogical tool for relating the characteristics of Yahweh and the religious ethos of the faith community. Though this is a variation from the examples recorded in the Pentateuch and Deuteronomistic History, the overall means of teaching through active learning remains unchanged in Wisdom Literature. Wisdom Literature relates the importance of adhering to the religious precepts of Yahweh through kinesthetic and visual instructional tools as well as social learning to assist learners with grasping the religious ethos of the instructor.

The use of the personification of Yahweh's wisdom through the character Wisdom in Proverbs 8 is a means for allowing the readers to "rediscover" their God as Creator through the observation of his work in creation itself. This use of observing creation affirms the distinct pedagogical feature of tangible images to reinforce religious ideals. Proverbs 8 directs readers to experience their God through experiencing creation. While the primary means of religious education was oral narrative relating accounts of Yahweh's actions on behalf of his people and the ensuing written record of these accounts, it is essential to identify the inclusion of visual cues such as the observations from nature, and the kinesthetic environments provided through the observations of others and active inquiry.

Previously published studies relating to education and the Hebrew Bible remain focused on the prevalence of formal education systems and supporting their existence. There remains little attention on pedagogy and how religious faith adherents are taught. While the didactive nature of scripture is uncontested, examinations of the teaching techniques preserved within these texts have predominantly remained overlooked.

CONTRIBUTION TO BIBLICAL RESEARCH

The primary purpose of this book is to highlight the interdisciplinary connection between active and social learning as it applies to examples of religious education described in the final canonical form of Wisdom Literature. To accomplish this task, I have focused on three areas:

educational theory, the social context for learning, and the biblical evidence for specific pedagogical features. The pedagogical features within Wisdom Literature directly align with the visual and kinesthetic learning identified in Neil Fleming's VARK learning theory as well as the social cognitive learning theory.

Wisdom is the search for the achievement of success through social and political harmony.[13] It is the ability to faithfully observe the religious laws even if it leads to one's demise. As described in Wisdom Literature, a wise man is not the man who achieves significant information about God or memorized the religious laws. Instead, the wise man is described as the one who can put these laws into practice in everyday choices. Wisdom is the ability to apply the law.

As the Israelites identify the orthodox practices for training the younger generations the means for accomplishing the self-discipline necessary for applying these religious laws, the writers took it upon themselves to record the means for achieving this ambitious virtue. Not only this, but they also recorded the means for continuing to teach the application of religious training. As weaknesses in choices and social activities are identified, writers emphasize them as well as how to choose correctly in accordance with the religious laws. This training then becomes preserved for future generations. In addition, the distinct illustrations from nature are recorded as well as the observations and testimonies from members of the community are also preserved as a means for formulating future pedagogical praxis.

Use of Nature as a Pedagogical Tool

The clearest example of the use of nature as a pedagogical tool is located in Job. Beginning with the emphasis from Elihu, "Who teaches like God" the focus of the text is centered on the instruction between Yahweh and Job. In his instructions, Yahweh uses nature as an illustration of his greatness as he teaches Job. He further builds his case as he references the sun and animals to further emphasize his sovereignty and unfathomable knowledge he uses in his governance over creation. This is used in contrast to Job's miniscule perspective. As the educator, Yahweh uses the magnitude and tangibility of the grandeur of nature to express to the learner what cannot be fully grasped without experiencing it. Without

---

13. Crenshaw, *Old Testament Wisdom*, 3.

Summary

perspective, the weak is misconceived as grand. However, as Job learns, his flawed perspective is reconfigured when given the influential illustration of Yahweh's vast knowledge and strength.

Proverbs likewise uses analogies derived from nature to explain the abstract. Prov. 26:1 draws a comparison from the weather to illustrate how honor to a fool is out of place. Likewise, Prov. 30:24–28 uses various insects and animals as illustrations for their desired traits of wisdom and strength within the social community. This is further illustrated in Proverbs 8 where wisdom is the agent Yahweh uses in creation. Here, wisdom is depicted as created first and is consequently present as creation unfolds through the architecture of Yahweh's command. As repeatedly depicted in Proverbs, the experiences of creation are parallel with experiencing the divine. Observations from nature carry theological implications. As shown in Prov. 8:22–31, It is Yahweh who creates, controls, and reveals. Therefore, creation itself points back to the Creator in an unprecedented illustration of his greatness and ongoing sovereign interaction.

Similarly to Job and Proverbs, Ecclesiastes depicts creation and the means by which Yahweh reveals himself to humanity. His masterful plan is beyond the conception of human imagination. However, its trustworthiness is mirrored in the consistency of the cycles and seasons portrayed in nature. Eccl. 1:3–7 uses the cycles of the sun, wind, and water to portray the reliability of the ongoing sequences of resources established by Yahweh. However, these cycles are impermanent in and of themselves. Their ultimate value derives from the role they play in the complete infrastructure of creation. This is used as illustration for the value of humanity. Each life and plan lacks ultimate meaning unless properly perceived within the full context of the full salvific plan of the Yahweh.

While the Song of Songs does use nature as a means for teaching, it does not use creation as a direct illustration for Yahweh's characteristics. Instead, nature is used as part of the powerful imagery describing the social interactions between the two main characters. Here, the imagery moves away from depicting God's sovereignty to depicting the emotion of the characters and evoking emotion from the reader.

Wisdom Literature is consistent in its use of nature as a visual illustration for teaching. With the exception of its use in the Song of Songs, it is used in combination with instructions on how it directly relates to Yahweh's attributes, revealing his character, reliability, sovereignty, and providence. Further, as noted in Proverbs, it reveals desired characteristics of humanity. In both cases, the overarching use of nature is as an illustration pointing the learner to the experiences gained from nature for the transference of knowledge from the experience to an abstract characteristic that cannot be experienced firsthand. Therefore, it becomes incumbent on the learner to connect how the experiences from creation directly relate to the revelation of the Creator through creation.

Use of Tradition as a Pedagogical Tool

The dialogues of the three friends reinforces their preoccupation with the religious traditions. Rather than assimilating the anomaly of Job's experiences with reason and inquiry, they obstruct his verbal defense with further resistance to change. Job's unexplainable suffering is repeatedly refuted as a direct result of disobedience, a theological perspective well rooted in Israelite tradition. They offer their friend no suggestions for his loss and physical agony. By the end of the first cycle of speeches, each of the three friends have invoked the widely-held consensus of Yahweh's greatness and his just punishment of the disobedient. In contrast, Job strongly counters and interjects that his friends cite beliefs, generalities, and opinions that are supported by nothing more than popularity. These, he protests, cannot overcome the undeniable facts of his personal experience.[14]

Like Job's friends, the father character in Proverbs draws on his expertise in tradition throughout his instructions to his son. He discusses the physical world and interactions of people through the lens of the cultural principles espoused through years of tradition. The expectation throughout the book of Proverbs is that the son will learn from these traditions advocated by his ancestors and community. In addition to the elders of the community, the father endorses his own teacher and sages as he communicates the traditions he has learned from both, as observed in Prov. 4:3–4. The collective observations of community, creation, and experience are part of the sapiential imagination passed on from teacher to learner. The memories and ongoing traditions are critical to the reflection and shaping of reality that defines the Israelites' rendering of Yahweh and his relationship with humanity.[15]

Similar to the father from Job, Qoheleth also teaches from his worldview that is shaped, in part, by tradition and experience. One of

14. Kushner, *Book of Job*, 88.
15. Perdue, *Wisdom*, 65.

the fundamental premises of his journey is to discover the meaning of life. While he seeks to explore through his philosophical inquiry, his use of tradition is undeniably intertwined and represented throughout his monologue that ultimately leads him to support the need to submit to the plan of the Creator.

The Song of Songs maintains its anomalies through this lack of incorporation of religious tradition. Its specific objective and content leads it to rely heavily on the poetic imagery that leaves little room for incorporating other material and teaching paradigms. It can certainly be argued that the courtship and wedding procession have a correlation with religious tradition. However, this begins to distract from the core role of the instructions of the text. The Song of Songs is not using the wedding procession as a pedagogical feature; therefore, it is not further discussed or included as a part of this study.

As a whole, the pattern for the use of tradition within the pedagogy of Wisdom Literature is part of the oral instruction. Unlike the Pentateuch and Deuteronomisitic History that relate to tradition in a direct and concrete portrayal of physical events and the festivals or monuments that authentic the testimony, Wisdom Literature simply refers to the sapiential knowledge of tradition. It is upheld as a source for wisdom based on the collective knowledge of tradition. It is sound because the elders themselves confirm its accuracy. Instead of tradition directly connected to events or locations, Wisdom Literature uses tradition as part of the oral aspect of the instructions. This tradition is then confirmed, not by remembering the event that led to the tradition, but the patterns and observations from nature that reinforce its truth. Therefore, by combining the oral instruction of tradition to the observations of creation, it moves the pedagogy from passive to active. Rather than simply giving the oral instructions along, they are combined with a second sense or means for learning; thereby maintaining the pattern of active learning. Additionally, Wisdom Literature also portrays the oral discussions of tradition as combined with the observations of social activity. This likewise too produces the pedagogy of active learning through the subcategory of social cognitive learning.

Use of Pentateuch as a Pedagogical Tool

Walter Brueggemann is correct as he discusses the role of "Torah-izing." In his discussion, he states that Torah has always functioned as the dominant source for religious content or literature. Unbothered by the extended generations who pull from it, it prevails through the anguish and cynicism of Job and Ecclesiastes. In every moment of the journey for Israel, the Torah has held the answers needed for the questions that arise.[16] It is from the traditions of the Torah, that every other text in the Hebrew Bible is derived. It is the Torah that the writers and editors of the other biblical books point back to. It is the foundation of the theological themes that permeate the other texts. It is therefore reasonable to look for these included examples that pull from the teachings of the Pentateuch in Wisdom Literature.

The two most prevalent Pentateuchal themes within Wisdom Literature is the focus on Yahweh as Creator and the contemplation of retributive theology from the Sinai Covenant and reaffirmed in Deuteronomy 28. Both of these themes are identified as early as Job 1 and 2. Within the framework of Job, Yahweh's sovereign governance over creation is affirmed through both the verbal exchanges between the characters as well as the illustrations used to demonstrate how Yahweh oversees the activities of beast and man. Directly relating to Yahweh's governance are the integrated themes of retribution and justice. Through the perspectives of the characters, the theological doctrine of salvation developed from the Pentateuch is also introduced. Through the three friends, Job is encouraged to repent so that the just punishments for his sins will be removed. From these exchanges, the readers learn that the friends make a direct correlation between Job's suffering and sin as guided by their interpretation of the religious laws. This ethos is directly challenged by Job. However, it is not his challenge to retributive theology that earns him the privilege of Yahweh's admonition; it is his challenge of Yahweh's justice. It should be noted that though the themes of the Pentateuch are represented in Job, with the exception of Yahweh as Creator, they are not necessarily used as pedagogical features.

This is also true of Ecclesiastes. Here, there is a strong reoccurring reference to creation and Yahweh as Creator. There are also references that reflect retributive theology and the laws of the Torah. However, it does not include specific references to events portrayed in the Pentateuch,

---

16. Brueggemann, *Creative Word*, 110.

including significant salvific events such as the exodus account. Likewise, Proverbs does not include references to the patriarchs, exodus event, or redemptive history. This also remains true for the Song of Songs.

Given these disparities, one must ask, what is the interrelation of these texts? Bernd Schipper and D. Andrew Teeter make a compelling case for the close association between Wisdom and Torah as a direct result of their extended editorial phases. Though distinct in their composition, they are similar in function. "Both represent to an equal degree compositions that rework and re-present scriptural material through an interpretive lens that is profoundly influenced and shaped by aspects of late wisdom tradition. This reworking is, in both cases, predicated upon a certain conception of the relationship between 'Wisdom' and Torah, or wisdom and the scriptural tradition more broadly."[17] There is wide scholarly agreement on the interrelated themes and contexts between Wisdom Literature and the Pentateuch. The themes and overall focus present many parallels between these two collections. Schipper and Teeter propose this may be largely influenced by their simultaneous editing stages within the exilic and post-exilic period. These parallels are supported here. However, the pedagogical features vary between these two collections. While both employ active learning, the Pentateuch uses concrete festivals, symbolism in religious attire, and monuments in combination with oral stories as part of the connection between physical and tradition. This is not the case in Wisdom Literature. Instead, Wisdom Literature uses nature and social activity in combination with instructions and testimony of observations as the connecting features that bridge the physical world and senses with tradition. Both collections include pedagogy that directly correlates with active learning but they arrive in two different means. As the Pentateuch is restoring the religious heritage of post-exilic Israel by anchoring the stories with concrete locations, it is arguable that Wisdom Literature is applying this religious heritage to daily activities and anchoring the instructions to observable patterns in the unchanging features of nature and social interactions.

Use of Social Context as a Pedagogical Tool

While there are undeniable parallels between Wisdom Literature and the Pentateuch, throughout this study, I have maintained that the two most

---

17. Schipper and Teeter, *Wisdom and Torah*, 235.

emphasized pedagogical features within Wisdom Literature is the use of nature and the use of social cognitive learning. Social cognitive theory, in particular, allows both the characters and readers to engage in active learning by observing the behaviors described in the texts as well as the positive and negative consequences in order to formulate a decision regarding the productivity of mimicking the actions observed/described.

It was argued in chapter 4 that Job presents the role of social cognitive learning in two ways. First, Job's three friends are presented with an opportunity to observe Job's actions and situation to either assimilate or accommodate their observations with their preunderstanding of the religious ethos and laws. Within the account, the three friends remain unchanged. It is Job who is central in the story as the learner. However, his primary change occurs through the concrete illustrations presented by Yahweh, not through observations of social activity. Therefore, this leads to the second use of social cognitive learning. Job himself embodies social learning for the readers as they recognize their affiliation in his character. The role of imagination through story reshapes experiences through the association and transference of the imagined to reality. Imagination constructs real ideas that are achievable. When used effectively in education, imagination does not ignore the facts of reality. Instead, it reconstructs the circumstances to create an imagined possibility that interacts with the facts of the situation. It was therefore contended in chapter 4 that the book of Job allows readers to identify with Job and place themselves alongside the characters of the text. Anchored to a historicized account of a man who cannot explain his circumstances, readers likewise move through the story with Job. As Job grapples with his grief and loss, he challenges the religious traditions that no longer make sense in light of his experiences. The readers also move through the story, imagining their own situation in the context of Job. Who can explain the unexplainable? Who can ask Yahweh humanity's greatest question, why? Through the account of Job, the unapproachable God enters to personally teach Job and thus also defend his justice and sovereign governance of creation to all readers whose hearts ache with grief and questions left unanswered. The pedagogical use of social cognitive learning in Job is a literary achievement that binds the concrete actions of the social community to address the impalpable questions that follow in the midst of grief.

The social cognitive learning in Proverbs occurs through the son's observations of members of the community. The destruction of the fool and reward for the wise are repeatedly iterated through the actions described in the text. Testimony and instruction are combined throughout the text to create the active learning pedagogy that is come to be expected in Wisdom Literature. The instructor moves back and for between describing his personal observations and giving further explanations for their significance and how the actions relate to Yahweh's expectations (and thus the social community's expectation) for the learner. Additionally, Proverbs uses the metaphor of the paths as a means for emphasizing the examples of the generations of elders who preceded the learner. The instructor stresses the importance of not learning from his own actions but to consider the ways of others and the outcomes of their choices. The expectation is that the learner will acquire knowledge and the ability to apply the religious laws to his daily life by watching his elders and choosing the path that leads to reward.

Like Proverbs, Ecclesiastes combines instruction with testimony. Here, the reader is also instructed to learn from the preceding generations. However, unlike Proverbs that emphasizes the reward of the elders who choose the correct path, Ecclesiastes emphasizes that the work of the elders ultimately fades away without memory in their death. The testimony of Qoheleth describes his observations of the social norms and the inferences he made toward his conclusions. He repeatedly challenges the ethos of reward for obedience as he claims that both the wise and fool die and their work is of no memory or value. He further asserts that humanity seeks God's wisdom but is too foolish to find it. In is discourse Qoheleth declares, human achievement is self-destructive, the memory of a man's life is forgotten in his death, human relationship is a delusion, and the short benefits of a man's life are squandered in his death. He focuses on the brevity of life and the disillusionment of achievement. These melancholy assertions lead Qoheleth to his masterful conclusion. The summation of his observation and examples of social cognitive learning lead him to deduce that value is ultimately found through Yahweh. Human achievement that exemplifies human effort is destructive while work that contributes to the plans of Yahweh are good. It is unimportant for a man to be remembered because it is Yahweh who is remembered for his work and governance of creation. Like Job, the social cognitive learning in Ecclesiastes occurs in two layers. First, Qoheleth himself learns by watching the behaviors of those around him. It is through these observations that Qoheleth derives his religious mythos. He then uses these observations in his testimony, leading to the second use of social cognitive learning. The suggestion is for his audience (and readers) to learn from his observations via his testimony of the accounts.

Finally, the Song of Songs is more similarly associated with Job's use of social cognitive learning. The audience is not encouraged to observe the behaviors of others nor does the writer describe his own observations per se. Instead, the Song of Songs portrays an account of two lovers whose relationship and emotion is described through the vivid poetical imagery. In support of Dewey's use of imagination in learning, like Job, the Song of Songs allows readers to experience the "story" alongside of the characters. Emotion is intangible and ultimately unrelatable until it is experienced. Therefore, the provocative use of imagery in Song of Songs invokes the senses and imagination of the reader that distinctly moves the learning into the framework of active learning through the observations of the characters and their portrayal of the heights and depths of emotion. The readers' marred concept of love is reconstructed through the experiences of the characters to produce a productive memory of love redefined.

In conclusion of this research, one of the primary pedagogical tools utilized in Wisdom Literature is the use of nature as an illustration for religious ethos. As communities are ravaged with change, Wisdom Literature relies on the steadfast cycles and features within nature as a pedagogical tool to instruct others about the steadfast ethos of Yahweh's provision, redemption, and plan. As Yahweh creates, he also restores. If he delivers the rising of the sun, he can assuredly deliver a community in need of hope.

The discussion regarding the timing of the editorial phases of Wisdom Literature remain ongoing, though the acceptance of the editing itself is largely uncontested. Texts such as Job highlight later editors' affirmation of the legitimacy of visual and tangible means of reinforcing oral religious instruction and offers support of the intentional inclusion of pedagogical ideals. The portrayal of Yahweh as Instructor is a significant text that reinforces the learning paradigm used by God himself as well as the intention to draw attention to Job's transformation through the instructions he received from Yahweh.

The authors and editors of Wisdom Literature persistently record their pedagogy alongside of their religious instructions to ensure the ongoing religious education that included visual and kinesthetic educational tools as well as social cognitive learning. Beyond the inherent didactic quality of the Hebrew Bible, pedagogical patterns are recorded and repeated throughout Wisdom Literature to decisively connect instruction to active learning models. As research has supported, instructions are not given in isolation. Instead, they are directly connected to an observable event such as nature or social behavior in order to reinforce the instructions through active experiential learning. Though different, this pattern is consistent with the teaching paradigm observed in the narratives of the Hebrew Bible where the pattern presented often includes "remember" (זָכַר, zakhar), "know" (יָדַע, yada'), and then a call to action such as keeping Yahweh's commandments as presented in Deut. 8:2.[18]

The pedagogical features described in Wisdom Literature can then be compared with the modern studies pertaining to learning theories and the psychology of learning. When these are compared, it is supported that there are two dominant teaching models used in Wisdom Literature. The first is visual learning combined with oral instruction. The second is social cognitive learning combined with oral instruction. The learners participate in the learning experience by actively engaging the visual learning achieved through the illustration or observed activity. Therefore, the learners engage in imagination and experiential learning that is used in combination with oral instructions. Lenore Borzak defines experiential learning as a, "direct encounter with the phenomena being studied rather than merely thinking about the encounter, or only considering the possibility of doing something about it."[19] Though it is over thirty years old, Borzak's definition of experiential learning continues in popularity and maintains its support in modern studies.[20] This conceptual framework of active/experiential learning through sight and imagery is transferrable to the examples illustrated within Wisdom Literature where the authors and editors include examples of instruction in order to the pedagogical tools to maintain their role in the ongoing religious training of younger generations.

Knowing Yahweh involves experiencing him but how does one experience the invisible and intangible. As the writers of Wisdom Literature seek to show, the fundamental characteristics of Yahweh are observable in creation itself. Is the power and authority of Yahweh questioned? Consider the mighty sea whose boundaries are controlled by him. The beasts of prey are themselves fed and cared for by him. Does one seek to

---

18. For my full discussion of the pedagogical patterns in the Pentateuch and Deuteronomistic History, cf. *Pedagogical Theory of the Hebrew Bible*.

19. Borzak, *Field Study*, 9.

20. Kolb, "David A. Kolb on Experiential Learning."

understand how something of insignificance can truly matter? Consider the ant who functions within its community to gather and collect. The one who works in isolation fails, unlike those who work together in unity of a single goal. Does one question the anomalies in one's life? Consider the cycles of the seasons. Though a single day may be an anomaly, the seasons return to their due course. In the same way that the learner can rely on the cycles and rhythms of nature, so Yahweh is reliable. The anomaly of a single event is feeble in the expanse of time and its interwoven connectivity to God's ultimate plan.

For later generations, these illustrations are preserved within the biblical texts as resources that reintroduce how to experience Yahweh. Though he is unseen, the providential control of God is clearly observed through creation. The significances of obedience and disobedience are perceived through the actions of the community surrounding the learner. One need not experience destruction to know its consequences. One need not search for God, for he surrounds the learner in the illustrations of his character. The narratives and poetry of Wisdom Literature allow the learner to relate to the ethos and mythos of the writers. The vigilant observations of creation and humanity animate the religious instructions girded in the traditions of the elders. Religious instructions are not mere monologues transferred to passive learners; the accounts come to life through the active involvement of the learner and the direct interaction between illustration, testimony, and teaching. The unimaginable becomes real, the intangible is touched, the invisible is seen, and the unknowable is experienced.

Bibliography

Acharya, S., and Shukla, S. "Mirror Neurons: Enigma of the Metaphysical Modular Brain. *Journal of Natural Science, Biology, and Medicine*, 3(2) (2012) 118–24.
Alter, Robert. *The Art of Biblical Poetry*. New York: Basic, 2011.
———. *The Wisdom Books: Job, Proverbs, and Ecclesiastes: A Translation with Commentary*. New York: Norton, 2010.
———. *Strong As Death Is Love: The Song of Songs, Ruth, Esther, Jonah, and Daniel, A Translation with Commentary*. New York: W.W. Norton & Company, 2016.
———. and Frank Kermode, eds. *The Literary Guide to the Bible*. Cambridge: Belknap Press, 1987.
Amit, Yairah. *Reading Biblical Narratives: Literary Criticism and the Hebrew Bible*. Translated by Yael Loten. Minneapolis: Fortress, 2001.
Atkinson, David. *The Message of Job*. Edited by J.A. Motyer. Downers Grove: InterVarsity, 1991.
Bandura, Albert. *Social Foundations of Thought and Action: A Social Cognitive Theory*. Englewood Cliffs, NJ: Prentice Hall, 1986.
———. "Social Cognitive Theory: An Agentic Perspective." *Asian Journal of Social Psychology*, 2 (1999) 21–41. https://www.uky.edu/~eushe2/Bandura/Bandura1999AJSP.pdf.
Bartholomew, Craig. *Ecclesiastes*. Grand Rapids: Baker Academic, 2009.
Bartholomew, Craig and Ryan O'Dowd. *Old Testament Wisdom Literature: A Theological Introduction*. Downers Grove: InterVarsity, 2011.
Berlin, Adele and Marc Zvi Brettler. "Psalms." In *The Jewish Study Bible*, edited by Adele Berlin and Marc Zvi Brettler, 1280–1446. New York: Oxford, 2004.
Berry, Donald. *An Introduction to Wisdom and Poetry of the Old Testament*. Nashville: Broadman and Holman, 1999.
Berquist, Jon L. "Childhood and Age in the Bible." *Pastoral Psychology* 58, no. 5/6 (2009) 521–30.
Biehler, Robert and Jack Snowman. *Psychology Applied to Teaching*. 5th ed. Boston: Houghton Mifflin, 1986.
Bleazby, Jennifer. "Imagination, Thinking and Education: The Use and Facilitation of the Imagination in the Philosophy for Children Classroom." Paper Presented at 3rd Global Conference (2007). http://inter-disciplinary.net/ati/education/cp/ce3/bleazby%20paper.pdf.

———. "Overcoming Relativism and Absolutism: Dewey's Ideals of Truth and Meaning in Philosophy for Children." *Educational Philosophy & Theory* 43, no. 5 (2011) 453–66.

Blenkinsopp, Joseph. "The Family in First Temple Israel." In *Families in Ancient Israel*, 48–103. Louisville: Westminster John Knox, 1997.

Bloch, Ariel, and Chana Bloch, trans. *The Song of Songs: The World's First Great Love Poem*. New York: Modern Library, 2006.

Bloomberg, Craig. "The Historical-Critical/Grammatical View." In *Biblical Hermeneutics: Five Views*, edited by Stanley Porter and Beth Stovell, 27–47. Downers Grove: InterVarsity, 2012.

Borzak, Lenore. *Field Study: A Source Book for Experiential Learning*. Beverly Hills: Sage, 1981.

Bray, Gerald. *Biblical Interpretation: Past and Present*. Downers Grove: InterVarsity, 1996.

Bromiley, Geoffrey, ed. "Education." *International Standard Bible Encyclopedia*, Electronic Database Biblesoft, 2006.

Brown, William. *Character in Crises*. Grand Rapids: Eerdmans, 1996.

———. *Ecclesiastes*. Louisville: Westminster John Knox, 2011.

Brueggemann, Walter. *An Introduction to the Old Testament: The Canon and Christian Imagination*. Louisville: Westminster John Knox, 2003.

———. *The Creative Word: Canon as a Model for Biblical Education*. Philadelphia, Fortress, 1982.

Bryant, Ian, Rennie Johnston, and Robin Usher. *Adult Education and the Postmodern Challenge: Learning Beyond the Limits*. New York: Routledge, 1997.

Caneday, Ardel B. "Qoheleth: Enigmatic Pessimist or Godly Sage?" *Grace Theological Journal* 7:1 (Spring 1986) 21–56.

Carroll, John. "Children in the Bible." *Interpretation* 55, 2 (2001) 121–34.

Callaway, Phillip. "Deut. 21:18–21: Proverbial Wisdom and Law." *Journal of Biblical Literature* 103, no. 3 (1984) 341–52.

Collins, John. "Wisdom Reconsidered, in Light of the Scrolls." *Dead Sea Discoveries* 4 (1997) 265–81.

Coogan, Michael. *A Brief Introduction to the Old Testament: The Bible In Its Context*, 3rd ed. New York: Oxford, 2016.

Constable, Thomas. "Notes on Ecclesiastes," *Expository Notes* (2016). http://soniclight.com/constable/notes/pdf/ecclesiastes.pdf.

Constable, Thomas. "Notes on Job." *Expository Notes* (2016). http://soniclight.com/constable/notes/pdf/job.pdf.

Crenshaw, James L. "Education in Ancient Israel." *Journal of Biblical Literature* 104 (1985) 601–15.

———. *Education in Ancient Israel: Across the Deadening Silence*. New York: Doubleday, 1998.

———. *Old Testament Wisdom: An Introduction*. Louisville, Westminster John Knox, 1998.

———. *Old Testament Wisdom: An Introduction*. 3rd ed. Louisville, Westminster John Knox, 2010.

Davis, Ellen. *Proverbs, Ecclesiastes, and the Song of Songs*. Louisville: Westminster John Knox, 2000.

Dell, Katharine. *The Book of Proverbs in Social and Theological Context.* Cambridge: Cambridge University Press, 2006.

Dewey, John. *Experience and Education.* 1938. Reprint, New York: Touchstone, 1997.

———. *How We Think.* 1910. Reprint, New York: Cosimo Classics, 2007.

———. *Reconstruction in Philosophy*, 1948. Reprint, New York: Dover, 2004.

Enns, Peter. *Ecclesiastes.* Grand Rapids: Eerdmans, 2011.

Estes, Daniel *Handbook on the Wisdom Books and Psalms.* Grand Rapids: Baker Academic, 2005.

———. *Hear My Son: Teaching and Learning in Proverbs 1—9*, ed. D. A. Carson. Downers Grove: Intervarsity, 2003.

Fenwick, Tara. *Learning Through Experience: Troubling Orthodoxies and Intersecting Question (Professional Practices in Adult Education and Lifelong Learning Theories).* Malabar, FL: Krieger, 2003.

Fleer, Marilyn. "The Cultural Construction of Child Development: Creating Institutional and Cultural Intersubjectivity." *International Journal of Early Years Education* 14, no. 2 (2006) 127–40.

Fletcher, Garth, and Julie Fitness. *Knowledge Structures in Close Relationships: A Social Psychological Approach.* New York: Psychology Press, 2014.

Fokkelman, J.P. *Reading Biblical Poetry: An Introductory Guide.* Translated by Ineke Smit. Louisville: Wesminster John Knox, 2001.

Fox, Michael V. "Ancient Near Eastern Wisdom Literature (Didactic)." *Religion Compass* 5, no. 1 (2011) 1–11.

———. *Proverbs.* New York: Doubleday, 2000.

———. "The Pedagogy of Proverbs 2." *Journal of Biblical Literature* 113, no. 2 (1994) 233–43.

Frymer-Kensky, Tikva. "Gender and Law: An Introduction." In *Gender and Law in the Hebrew Bible and Ancient Near East.* 97–112. Sheffield: Sheffield Academic, 1998.

Furnham, Adrian. *The Psychology of Behaviour At Work: The Individual In the Organization.* Hove, East Sussex: Psychology, 2005.

Gage, N.L., and David Berliner. *Educational Psychology.* 3rd ed. Boston: Houghton Mifflin, 1984.

Gardner, Howard. *Frames of Mind: The Theory of Multiple Intelligences.* New York: Basic, 1993.

Garroway, Kristine Henriksen. *Children in the Ancient Near Eastern Household.* Winona Lake, IN: Eisenbrauns, 2014.

Gerhardsson, Birger. *Memory and Manuscript with Tradition and Transmission in Early Christianity.* Translated by Eric Sharpe. Grand Rapids: Eerdmans, 1998.

Gese, Hartmut. "Wisdom Literature in the Persian Period." In *Cambridge History of Judaism*, vol. 1, *The Persian Period,* edited by W.D. Davies and Louis Finkelstein, 189–218. Cambridge: Cambridge University Press, 1984.

Gillespie, Mary. "Student–teacher Connection: A Place of Possibility." *Journal of Advanced Nursing* 52, no. 2 (2005) 211–19.

Goff, Matthew. "Qumran Wisdom Literature and the Problem of Genre." *Dead Sea Discoveries* 17 (2010) 315–35.

Good, Carter V. ed., *Dictionary of Education.* New York: McGraw-Hill, 1945.

Hagglund, S. et al. "Early Childhood Education and Learning for Sustainable Development and Citizenship." *International Journal of Early Childhood* 41(2) (2009) 49–63.

Harris, R. Laird, et al., eds. *Theological Word Book of the Old Testament*. Chicago: Moody, 1980.

Hayes, Katherine. *Proverbs*. Collegeville: Liturgical, 2016.

Hayes, Nóirín. "Children's Rights—Whose Right? A Review of Child Policy Development in Ireland." *Studies in Public Policy* 9 (2002) Dublin: The Policy Institute at Trinity College Dublin. Available at: http://www.tcd.ie/policy-institute/assets/pdf/BP9_Children_Hayes.pdf

Hess, Richard. *Song of Songs*. Edited by Tremper Longman III. Grand Rapids: Baker Book House, 2005.

Honeck, Richard. *A Proverb in Mind: The Cognitive Science of Proverbial Wit and Wisdom*. Mahwah, NJ: Lawrence Erlbaum Associates, 1997.

Hubbard, David. *Ecclesiastes, Song of Solomon*. Dallas: Word Books, 1991.

Hunt, Patrick. *Poetry in the Song of Songs: A Literary Analysis*. New York: Peter Lang, 2008.

Jarvis, Peter. *Twentieth Century Thinkers in Adult Education (International Perspectives on Adult Education)*. New York: Routledge, 1987.

_____ and Stella Parker. *Human Learning: A Holistic Approach*. New York: Routledge, 2006.

Jenks, Chris. *Childhood*. London: Routledge, 1996.

Johnston, Gordon H. "The Enigmatic Genre and Structure of the Song of Songs, Part 3." *Bibliotheca Sacra* 166:663 (2009) 289–305.

Kaiser, Walter C., Jr. *Ecclesiastes: Total Life*. Everyman's Bible Commentary. Chicago: Moody, 1979.

Keopf-Taylor, Laurel. *Give Me Children or I Shall Die: Children and Communal Survival in the Biblical World*. Minneapolis: Augsburg Fortress, 2013.

Knowles, Malcolm. *The Modern Practices of Adult Education: From Pedagogy to Andragogy*. Englewood Cliffs: Cambridge, 1980.

Kolb, David. *Experiential Learning: Experience as the Source of Learning and Development*, 1st Ed. New York: Pearson FT, 1984.

Kraus, Donald. *The Book of Job: Annotated and Explained*. Skylight Paths, 2012.

Kushner, Harold. *The Book of Job: When Bad Things Happen to a Good Person*. New York: Schocken, 2012.

Larrimore, Mark. *The Book of "Job": A Biography*. Woodstock: Princeton University, 2013.

Lewis, Jack. "Jamnia Revisited." In *The Canon Debate*, edited by Lee Martin McDonald and James Sanders, 146–62. Peabody: Hendrickson, 2002.

Li, M.P. and B.H. Lam. "Cooperative Learning." *The Active Classroom*. The Hong Kong Institute of Education, 2013. http://www.ied.edu.hk/aclass/Theories/cooperativelearningcoursewriting_LBH%2024June.pdf.

Longman III, Tremper. *Job*. Grand Rapids: Baker Academic, 2012.

_____. *Proverbs*. Grand Rapids: Baker Academic, 2006.

Lucas, Earnest. *Exploring the Old Testament: A Guide to the Psalms and Wisdom Literature*, vol. 3. Downers Grove: InterVarsity, 2003.

Machinist, Peter. "Ecclesiastes." In *The Jewish Study Bible*, edited by Adele Berlin and Marc Zvi Brettler, 1603–1622. New York: Oxford, 2004.

Matthews, Victor. "Honor and Shame in Gender Related Legal Situations in the Hebrew Bible." In *Gender and Law in the Hebrew Bible and Ancient Near East*. 97–112. Sheffield: Sheffield Academic, 1998.

Merriam, Sharan, et al. "Experience and Learning." In *Learning in Adulthood: A Comprehensive Guide*, 159–88. Hoboken: Wiley, 2007.

———. "Knowles's Andragogy, and Models of Adult Learning by Mcclusky, Illeris, and Jarvis." In *Learning in Adulthood: A Comprehensive Guide*, 83–104. Hoboken: Wiley, 2007.

McKane, William. *Proverbs: A New Approach*. London: SCM, 1970.

McMillion, Phillip. "Psalm 78: Teaching the Next Generation." *Restoration Quarterly* 43, No. 4 (2001) 219–28.

Mikulincer, Mario. *Human Learned Helplessness: A Coping Perspective*. The Springer Series in Social Clinical Psychology. New York, Springer, 2014.

Millard, Allen R. "The Question of Israelite Literacy." *Bible Review* 3:3 (Fall 1987) 22–31.

Moloney, Katherine. "Pedagogy of Social Transformation in the Hebrew Bible: Allowing Scripture to Inform Our Interpretive Strategy for Contemporary Application." *HTS Theological Studies* vol. 72 no. 3 (2016).

Mortimore, Peter. *Understanding Pedagogy: and its Impact on Learning*. London: SAGE, 1999.

Neufeld, Henry. "Psalm 104: God—Creator and Sustainer." http://rpp.energion.com/psalm104.shtml.

O'Connor, Kathleen. *The Wisdom Literature*. Collegeville, MT: Michael Glazier, 1990.

Omrode, Jeanne. *Human Learning*, 5th ed. New York: Pearson, 2007.

Parker, Julie Faith. "You are a Bible Child: Exploring the Lives of Children and others through the Elisha Cycle." In *Women in the Biblical World: A Survey of the Old and New Testament Perspectives*, 59–70. Lanham, MD: University Press of America, 2009.

Perdue, Leo. *Wisdom Literature: A Theological History*. Louisville: Westminster John Knox, 2007.

Peterson, David. "Genesis and Family Values." *Journal of Biblical Literature* 124 (2005) 5–23.

Rowley, H.H., *The Book of Job*. New Century Bible Commentary. Grand Rapids: Eerdmans, 1981.

Schipper, Bernd, and D. Andrew Teeter, eds. *Wisdom and Torah: The Reception of 'Torah' in the Wisdom Literature of the Second Temple Period*. Leiden: Brill, 2013.

Shepherd, Gerald. *Wisdom as a Hermeneutical Construct: A Study in the Sapientializng of the Old Testament*. Berlin: de Gruyter, 1980.

Siegel, Daniel J. *The Developing Mind: Toward a Neurobiology of Interpersonal Experience*. New York: Guilford, 1999.

Smith, Gary. "Is There a Place for Job's Wisdom in Old Testament Theology?" *Trinity Journal* 13NS (1992) 3–20.

Smyth, Marie. "The Concept of Childhood and the Experience of Children in Violently Divided Societies." In *Childhood and Its Discontents: The First Seamus Heaney Lectures*, edited by J. Dunne and J. Kelly, 159–97. Dublin: Liffey, 2003.

Sneed, Mark. "Job." In *The Transforming Word*, edited by Mark Hamilton. Abilene: Abilene Christian University Press, 2009.

Steignberg, Naomi. *The World of the Child in the Hebrew Bible*. Sheffield: Sheffield Phoenix, 2013.

Stern, Elsie. "Song of Songs." *The Jewish Study Bible*. Edited by Adele Berlin and Marc Zvi Brettler New York: Oxford, 2004.

Strauss, Valarie. "Howard Gardner: 'Multiple Intelligences' are not 'Learning Styles.'" *Washington Post* (2013). https://www.washingtonpost.com/news/answer-sheet/wp/2013/10/16/howard-gardner-multiple-intelligences-are-not-learning-styles/ (accessed April 24, 2014).

Tan, Nancy Nam Hoon. *The "Foreignness" of the Foreign Woman in Proverbs 1—9: A Study of the Origin and development of a Biblical Motif.* Berlin: de Gruyter, 2008.

Van der Zwan, Peter. "Song of Songs: A Celebration of and Invitation to Participate in the Fullness of Life." *Verbum et Ecclesia* 36.3 (2015) 1–6.

Van Gog, Tamara, et al. "The Mirror Neuron System and Observational Learning: Implications for the Effectiveness of Dynamic Visualizations." *Educational Psychology Review* 21, no. 1 (2009) 21–30.

Von Rad, Gerhard. *Wisdom in Israel.* Nashville: Abingdon, 1972.

Vygotsky, Lev. "Pedagogy of the Adolescent." *The Collected Works of L.S. Vygotsky.* Volume 5: Child Psychology, edited by R. W. Rieber, 31–184. New York: Plenum, 1998.

Walton, John, and Andrew Hill. *Old Testament Today: A Journey from Original Meaning to Contemporary Significance.* Grand Rapids, Zondervan, 2004.

Weeks, Stuart. *Instruction and Imagery in Proverbs 1—9.* Oxford: Oxford University Press, 2007.

Weinfeld, Moshe. *Deuteronomy 1—11.* 1st ed. Anchor Bible. New York: Doubleday, 1991.

Whybray, R.N. *The Intellectual Tradition in the Old Testament.* Berlin: de Gruyter, 1974.

———. *Proverbs.* Grand Rapids: Eerdmans, 1994.

Winnicott, Donald W. *Playing and Reality.* London: Tavistock, 1971.

Wyler, Robert. *Handbook of Social Cognition,* vol. 2. 2nd ed. New York: Psychology, 2014.

Yount, William. *Created to Learn: A Christian Teacher's Introduction to Educational Psychology.* Nashville: Broadman & Holmes, 1996.

www.ingramcontent.com/pod-product-compliance
Lightning Source LLC
Chambersburg PA
CBHW071506150426
43191CB00009B/1433